SHATTERED DREAMS.

A Three-Pronged Injustice

Lies
Family Greed
Guardianships

PAM TRAINOR

Cover photograph, Remnants of a Short Pier
by: Pam Trainor
Copyright © Pam Trainor

Shattered Dreams: A Three-Pronged Injustice
Copyright © 2023 by Pam Trainor

All rights reserved.

Permission to reproduce in any form
must be secured from the author.

Disclaimer. This work depicts actual events in the life of the author and is based on the personal recollection, documentation, and public court records of the cases regarding the protagonist, "Pam." To protect the privacy of those depicted, some names of individuals have been changed. Some of the dialogues created by the author are rooted in public documents and signed affidavits by witnesses in the court cases. Any cautionary suggestions made in the book are not intended as legal advice to the readers.

FOREWORD

"My reaction as a retiree to this story is shock and some trepidation at how easy it is for greedy, unscrupulous relatives to isolate an elder and then blame a good-hearted friend who had been assisting her and cause her jailing for exploitation. The collusion of incompetent police officers, corrupt prosecutors, shady lawyers and dull-witted social service workers shows that all elders and those who help them have a target on their backs because our broken Justice and Guardianship systems protect the guilty and punish the innocent.

This genre-busting account is a tragedy, a true crime story, a chronicle of human and civil rights violations and a manual for protecting elders from predatory relatives. If it were not a true story it would be too unbelievable a tale to tell. Essential reading for retirees and those who assist them in their declining years." *Retired Teacher, Baltimore, MD.*

****

We enter a world where the elder is vulnerable and the compass points of right and wrong can be distorted. The story unfolds with an acute desire to draw readers into the story where they might ask fundamental questions about justice. If anyone needs an illustration of the adage — "No good deed goes unpunished"— read this book. *Retired Educational Administrator, Baltimore, MD*

HNR PRESS
P.O. Box 9857
Towson, MD 21284
202-856-7624

Contact@hnrpress.org

All Rights Reserved. First Edition 2023

Printed in the United States of America

1 2 3 4 5 6 7 8 9 10

This book is dedicated to all those wrongfully stripped of their civil rights, maliciously isolated, and financially ruined by others claiming to be a loving family member, a family member who lies to conceal their true motive.

CONTENTS

Preface

As far back as I can remember, I would periodically find lost dogs in my neighborhood and return them to their owners. I grew up in a small cul-de-sac of about twenty houses, surrounded by two other communities, all were single family homes. It wasn't unusual for a family pet to jump a fence or sneak out a door. Back in the 60's and 70's, kids roamed the neighborhoods going from one yard to the next on a daily basis. If I spied a loose dog, I'd befriend it, bring it home, give it water and check its tags for a phone number, and call its owner to tell them their pet was safe.

I can still recall several of the pups whom I returned to their owners, but one in particular stands out. Maybe he stands out because it was the last dog I would bring home. On that day, I brought home a fully grown, male Doberman Pinscher. I thought nothing of it, since I just loved all dogs, and he was obviously lost. To my surprise, my parents refused to come outside onto the front porch where I was giving him water. They merely instructed me to read the phone number off the dog's tag, so that they could call the owner.

I remember the owner, a tall thin man, repeatedly telling my parents how gentle the Doberman was, and how upset he was not knowing where to look for his dog. He was grateful that we had cared for his buddy until he could arrive to pick him up. In a sense, I was grateful for the Doberman too, as my parents surprised me shortly thereafter with my own dog. I'm guessing they didn't want anymore Dobermans on their front porch.

I don't know what prompted this empathy for lost dogs and their owners. For years, I remembered how good it felt, seeing the joy of them being reunited with each other. That good feeling encouraged me to repeat acts of kindness to friends and strangers who were in need.

It might have been helping a neighbor carry groceries into their home, helping a friend fix a broken bicycle, or helping a relative with yard work.

During my high school years at Notre Dame Prep, my desire to help others was encouraged by the school's philosophy of social outreach. In the hearts of its students was the Prophet Micah's call to "act justly, to love tenderly, and to walk humbly with God" (Micah 6:8). This invitation to answer God's call had been in the school's mission statement for years. Its social service program reached out to people in need, nearby and afar. I embraced that philosophy and decided that I would always try to give a helping hand to someone in trouble. Helping others became a part of my DNA.

In hindsight, it should not be surprising that, in my adult life, I chose to volunteer as a firefighter and auxiliary police officer. At one point, inspired by the nuns who taught me, I even considered becoming a nun so that I could dedicate my whole life to helping others. It was at this point, in my 20s, I was "diagnosed" as co-dependent on helping others. It has always bothered me that someone would see wanting to help others as a character flaw, described as "co-dependent."

And now, in middle age, I am facing the greatest challenge that ever emerged from my lifelong habit of helping people in need. Not only did I fail in my quest to protect a friend from being exploited by her family, but I have been portrayed as a heinous criminal and pursued by law enforcement in one of the most unforeseeable series of events ever imagined. My friend is now in an assisted living facility against her will, and I am still fighting to find justice and regain my reputation after spending time in jail for elder exploitation.

To justify what I did and to expose the massive, for-profit guardianship system in this country, I felt the need to write this memoir. It shows how close relatives can use police, lawyers, doctors, and courts to obtain guardianship and control the life of an aging relative, place that relative in a protective facility, and separate them from their hard-earned investments and possessions, thus preventing them from enjoying the retirement they had dreamed of for years. In the process, other protectors sometimes become a target.

In our rapidly aging population, thousands are joining the population of seniors on any given day. Hordes are lying in wait to steal their hard-earned assets and take away their civil rights. I hope that my memoir will be a warning that "the wolf is at your door"[1] or the door of someone you care about.

Someone reading this story might think that I have a definite self-interest in sharing it: it sounds like an "*oratio pro domo*"—a plea in my own interest. Of course, I want to show that I was innocent of the charges of elder financial abuse. I was furious when my 2019 lawyer announced in the presence of my friend, "Your accusers have to prove you're guilty; I don't have to prove you're innocent."

Although I am writing this memoir, the story is not primarily about me, but about a woman who was dreaming of spending the rest of her life in a North Carolina vacation home with her lifelong friend. The loss of her friend changed everything. Dorothea's retirement dream vanished completely when family members and courts decided that she should spend her retirement in an assisted living facility as a guardianship Ward.

The following court cases provided publicly accessible documentation used to research and write this story:

2015- Orange Co. FL 2015-DR-01910-3-0 Dissolution Marriage

2018- Orange Co. FL 2018 TR-020766-A-W Traffic

---

[1] See Michael Hackard, Esq. *The Wolf Is at the Door. Undue Influence and Elder Financial Abuse.* Hackard Global Media, LLC, 2017. This work gives excellent warnings and tips on how to protect relatives and loved ones against possible abusers of the elderly.

2019- Brunswick Co. NC 19CR-052909 Criminal

2019- Baltimore Co. MD D-08-FM-19-007414 EMV

2019- Baltimore Co. MD DO-8CR-1900653 Felony Warrant

2019- Brunswick Co. NC 19SP270 Incompetency Hearing

2019- Orange Co. FL 2019-GA-00283-0 Guardianship of Person
        and Property

2022- Baltimore MD 22-CV-1505-GLR Defamation

Prologue

I am Pam, a single woman in my mid-fifties who befriended my former high school teacher Dorothea after she lost her lifelong friend Mary Anne to brain cancer. They had planned to retire in the house they built in Sunset Beach, North Carolina. Dorothea was devastated by the loss of her friend and was now facing a life of loneliness and the challenges of aging. Having helped people throughout my life, I offered Dorothea my assistance. For almost two years I helped her prepare for her dreamed retirement in North Carolina.

Over the years, Dorothea's family had kept only sporadic contact with her. But they became suspicious of my motivations and thought that I was after the considerable financial assets Dorothea had inherited from her friend. Dorothea's sister, brother, and nephew put together a series of unsubstantiated allegations against me that resulted in my arrest and jail time for "exploitation of the elderly." With the assistance of lawyers, the police, and the guardianship courts in North Carolina and Florida, the family obtained guardianship over Dorothea and placed her in an assisted living facility in Florida against her will. They now have unbridled access to all her assets, and Dorothea has lost all her civil rights.

For the last two years, I have been fighting felony charges against me in court. The assistant district attorney and the courts have kept delaying hearings and asking for continuances. Justice delayed is justice denied! In the meantime, I have been unable to contact Dorothea. I keep hoping that her stay in the assisted living facility will only be temporary.

What happened to Dorothea and to me is just one example of what is happening in the broken and corrupt guardianship system, which sometimes appoints guardians, in many cases family members, whose motivations are not entirely pure. Instead of making sure that the Wards are taken care of when they cannot take care of themselves, the Wards are used for the guardians' financial benefit. It is estimated that the United States has about 1.5 million active guardianships, in control over more than $1 billion of combined assets. The quotation of St. Jerome's Latin Vulgate is quite appropriate here: *Radix omnium malorum est cupiditas.* The root of all evil is greed.

This story is a real-life experience about the multiple pitfalls of the guardianship system in this country. It is also a warning to anyone who is trying to help a person in need. So extreme caution is warranted if you want to assist an elderly person.

Thinking that my story would be beneficial to people who help elders or who are involved in guardianships, I relied on a former colleague, a teacher and author, to help me present the facts without an emotional bias. After doing hours of interviews and receiving thousands of pages of documentation from me, he mentored and coached me to bring this book to fruition. He advised me on what materials to include and how best to present them.

This narrative presents a timeline of the events experienced by Dorothea and me, and explains the road her family took to obtain guardianship. In addition, I provide some valuable insights into the pitfalls of the guardianship system in America. In the epilogue I asked my mentor to reflect on what he personally learned from this experience.

I do hope that *Shattered Dreams: A Three-Pronged Injustice,* awakens people about the perils of the guardianship system, which is in dire need of reform at both the state and the national level. Dorothea's and my stories are repeated at an alarming rate among the rapidly aging population of the United States.

April 1980: A Teacher and a Friend

In sharing my story, I hope to reach someone who needs to know more about guardianships. Perhaps that someone has a relative who was ordered to have a guardian; or, that someone has an aging aunt who is losing her ability to make rational decisions and does not know what to do. I want to expose the pitfalls of the guardianship system and warn everybody that, "the wolf is at the door."

I got to know Miss Dorothea when I was a junior at Notre Dame Prep, a Catholic high school for girls. One Tuesday morning, after Assembly, in Miss Dorothea's U.S. History class, seventeen pairs of eyes were focused on me. I was tasked with getting Miss Dorothea off her planned topic at the beginning of the class with a question about a current event that I had read about in the newspaper that morning. All my classmates were wondering if I would again try to steer the teacher off track.

From the first days I had Miss Dorothea as my teacher, I always felt that she reflected a commanding presence of authority. In her mid-thirties, she was average in stature. Her hair, had a slight wave, was parted in the middle and covered her forehead on just one side, otherwise framing her round face. It was a conservative style among the massive, teased hairdos of the 80's, a hold-over from the 60's. But her hazel eyes, behind her glasses, and her perpetual mysterious smile, always seemed to tell the story. Before saying anything to you, her eyes would stare at you for a few moments. When looking for a thought or when lost in thought she would tilt her head to the left. You knew something unexpected was coming. She was never dressed in flashy colors but seemed to prefer conservative outfits with subdued shades, not unlike many of the female teachers at the private school, in that manner, she fit right in.

That Tuesday morning Miss Dorothea walked into class, holding her usual cup of dark roasted coffee. I was ready.

"Miss Dorothea, what do you think about the Ayatollah Khomeini, who let students take fifty-two U.S. Embassy staff as hostages in Tehran? They claim that America can't do a darn thing about them. Should Carter try to liberate them?"

After staring for a minute at me, her typical mysterious smile came over her face. She took a sip of her coffee. "Well, Pam, I see that you fulfill the expectation of your classmates to get me off topic again, but I will comment on what you asked because it is an important moment in our history."

I made an apologizing gesture but glanced around for the approving smiles of my classmates. Miss Dorothea began an extended commentary on the Iran situation that lasted about half of class time. I had done it again!

Miss Dorothea had been used to my antics. But she was a no-nonsense history teacher who was convinced that the young women in her classroom needed to know history. She subscribed to George Santayana's famous quote: "Those who cannot remember the past are condemned to repeat it."

I was the kind of student who routinely floated through classes with the least possible effort. I hated repetition, and reading textbooks after a class lecture, bored me so I would only "hit the books" to prepare for tests and quizzes. To my chagrin, some of my teachers thought I was a daydreamer who would overwhelm anyone with an avalanche of gray matter and what-ifs. Their recurring criticism was that I was rather inattentive and careless.

Satisfied with being a C-average student, without any thought of its impact on my future, my carefree attitude, insight and sense of humor

14

afforded me to hang with the top 10% of my classmates, who actually did study, and get good grades. Maybe I secretly hoped for some sort of good grade osmosis to occur. But I excelled in the arts and athletics. I loved painting and playing basketball, field hockey, and lacrosse. Most days I came to school in the team uniform, inviting comments from friends: "Do you ever wear the actual Notre Dame Prep dress?"

Since the school's founding in the late 19th century, the School Sisters of Notre Dame had focused on the education of girls. They were known for the academic and spiritual training of their students. After Vatican II, they expanded their two pillars of educational and spiritual goals, adding a third pillar: social justice. They developed a social service program that reached out to the local community and to communities abroad and taught the girls that caring for their fellow human beings was part of being a Catholic.

That was right up my alley. Although I was very much aware that my blue uniform and saddle shoes identified me as one of the girls from "the valley," Notre Dame's social outreach program taught me that caring for the underprivileged was a goal I could make my own as well.

Dorothea had been a history teacher at the high school for several years and was chair of the history department. She was very intelligent and had the reputation of being an excellent teacher. She had high standards and challenged her students to get to the heart of the matter. She was demanding but fair and always gave struggling students a second chance. Students knew they couldn't slide by or slack off. As the department chair, she taught the upper level and AP classes. Looking back, it was probably a scheduling error that required her to teach my mid-level class that year.

Her colleagues knew she had an uncanny insight into American and European history, and she could easily participate in discussions on a range of subjects: religion, art and literature, economics, and politics. One of her hobbies was reading books, and she absorbed their content exceptionally well. Her avid habit of watching TV news and reading newspapers kept her informed about international and American politics.

I personally experienced Miss Dorothea's fairness in the third quarter of my junior year. Miss Dorothea had given her pupils independent study for the entire quarter with a final test at the end. As usual, I had blown off the work until the night before the test. The one-on-one oral test became a disaster. Miss Dorothea was kind enough to give me a D without embarrassing or degrading me. But I had learned the best lesson of my high school years: one cannot get a good grade if one waits to study until the day before a test. I was fortunate to learn this before going to college.

Everybody at the school knew that Miss Dorothea had a close friend who lived with her, Miss Mary Anne. She taught Spanish and had been my homeroom teacher in my sophomore year. But I had first gotten to know Miss Mary Anne in my freshman year, when she pointed at me walking down the hall one day. "I know you!" she said. "You play basketball." My brother Tom coaches you. I usually go to the games and I've seen you play." To an athlete, being recognized by someone you don't know, is a big deal. It feels good. The exchange stuck with me over the years.

It was only later that I learned about the friendship between Miss Dorothea and Miss Mary Anne. The fact that they shared a house together led to all kinds of speculations and gossip: were they a couple? If they were, how could a Catholic school tolerate such a relationship? More charitable people looked at their relationship and saw two close friends who had decided to share the challenges of life together. And that was that!

After graduating in 1981 up until 2017, Dorothea and I had had only sporadic contact. Sporadic in this case is not insignificant as it was a school of only 500 students. It has always been a tight knit community. A year out of college, I was hired as the art teacher at Notre Dame Prep

Middle School for a couple years, and coached JV field hockey and JV lacrosse teams in the Upper School. Dorothea and I became co-workers. Years later, during a Career Day, I had been asked to speak to students on how to think creatively to get hired. I explained how my art skills in sculpture got me hired by a Department of Defense contractor and how I moved through the company from a toolbox worker to a department head. Our dynamics had changed again, as I was one of the speakers, and Dorothea was the moderator for the group of girls in the classroom.

It didn't end there, I also had contact with the school as an auxiliary police officer. I was frequently detailed as a security officer for events at Notre Dame Prep.

I would occasionally meet up with former Notre Dame Prep classmates, but I never participated in class reunions or other events at the school except when my auxiliary police officer's duties required it.

No matter how my relationship with Notre Dame Prep ebbed and flowed after I graduated, returning to the area always brought a sense of welcome and community. Miss Dorothea's history classes remained in my mind as enjoyable, and time well spent.

May 2017: The Month It All Changed

One Sunday in early May 2017, I was playing with my dogs when I got a text on my phone. It was an emergency medical services (EMS) text directed to the volunteer fire station I had been associated with for the last seven years. The text explained that a 69-year-old female with a brain tumor had fallen in her tub.

"Hey Mom, do you know any female about sixty-nine in Glen Arm with a brain tumor?" Having lived her whole life in Maryland and worked for twenty years at Loyola College, my mother had lots of contacts in Baltimore.

"No, why do you ask?"

"No special reason. This information came through an EMS text alert, and I thought you might know the person."

A week or so later, I received a call from an old high school friend. "Hello Pam, were you ever taught by Miss Dorothea or Miss Mary Anne at Notre Dame?"

"Yes, Dorothea was my history teacher in junior year, and I had Mary Anne as a homeroom teacher in sophomore year. Why do you ask?"

"Miss Mary Anne died. She had a brain tumor." In a flash I thought of the EMS text I had received.

"Are you going to the wake and the funeral? Perhaps we can go together?" my friend asked.

"I don't know," I replied. "Let's see when and where they will take place and I'll be in touch with you."

Throughout the day, images of Mary Anne's homeroom and Dorothea's classes kept appearing in my head. In the almost forty years since I graduated, some Notre Dame Prep faculty members had died, but I had never attended any of their funerals. I had good memories of Dorothea as a teacher and colleague. She might appreciate my presence at the wake or funeral. Furthermore, since Mary Anne's brother Tom had been my basketball coach, attending his sister's funeral would be a sign of respect. I had an odd feeling that I was supposed to go to this wake. I did not know exactly why, but I sensed that I had to be there.

Arriving at the wake, I immediately recognized teachers, co-workers, and classmates from my days at Notre Dame Prep. As I stood before the casket, memories of Mary Anne dismissing her homeroom students at three o'clock went through my head. They were intermingled with images of Mary Anne rooting for our basketball team. I felt sad that Mary Anne had so suddenly been taken away from her best friend Dorothea.

When I turned around, Dorothea was standing off to the right of me. She stared at me for a few moments, her head tilting slightly to the left, and said, "I know I'm supposed to know you, but I can't remember your name."

"You taught me U.S. History at Notre Dame Prep in the 80's. Mary Anne was my sophomore homeroom teacher, and her brother Tom was my basketball coach. You might remember the Career Day where I had the girls don a welder's jacket, gloves and helmet. You were the class moderator."

Her eyes lit up. "Ah, now I remember," Dorothea said with a faint smile. "You're Pam, the one who tried to get me off topic every day at the start of class, by asking my opinion on a topic you had seen in the newspaper. I think I enjoyed the discussion as much as you enjoyed getting me off topic. That was quite a few years ago!"

"Yes! That would be me, Dorothea," I said, acknowledging my shenanigans in her classroom. "I am so sorry that you have lost your best friend, Mary Anne. You know, I'm a volunteer with the fire company that responded to your home that day. I wasn't at the fire house when the 911 was received, but I did get the EMS text message about it. I never associated it with you though until someone told me about Mary Anne. I'm sorry." Dorothea appeared a little distant as she quietly replied, "There were so many firefighters and police." However, she snapped right back, looked at me, squinted, and said, "I remember you taught in the Middle School too, didn't you?" Surprised that she had remembered, I replied, "Yes! Yes, I did. Hey, listen, if you ever need any help don't hesitate to call me. I can do all kinds of things from computer and home repairs to yard work." I gave her my email address and cell phone number.

"Thank you, Pam, that's a very nice offer. I'll be okay. But perhaps one day we could go out and have lunch and reminisce about the old days," she suggested.

"That's a wonderful idea," I replied, giving her a hug.

"By the way, you mentioned that you know Mary Anne's brother. Tom. He is right over there. Let's go and talk to him."

As we got closer, Tom looked our way and I grinned and said, "Tommy!" Tom went with the flow and flashed a sheepish grin. "How do I know you?" I said, "Well, your sister taught me in high school, but you wouldn't know me from that. I was so sorry to hear Mary Anne passed. I'm sorry for your loss. She was such caring person." Tom glanced down. "Thank you, she was a very special person, a one of a kind. She will be missed." He paused, "Now don't tell me who you are, let me guess." I replied, "Okay, there were 12 of us," was my first clue. "Was it on the west side of town?" Tom asked. "No. It was right next door at the school." I could tell the wheels were spinning, but keep in mind this was 40 years ago. I added, "Danny and Charlie were involved." Which was kind of a lame clue since the three boys were like brothers from a different mother, and were always together. Tom's searching, searching for memories, "one more clue." Okay, Mona (a classmate from 1st grade to 12th, and the little sister of Danny and Charlie) was one of the 12. Tom blurts out "Basketball!" "Yes! I'm..." I can't even finish my sentence before Tom excitedly announces, "TRAINOR! You were our whole team! Let's get a photo. I want to send it to Danny, who's in California." I found myself stumbling over my words. We had a lot of fun on the team, and the guys had devised some specific plays...because of my height advantage, but I don't think it was necessarily because of any skill I possessed. I was surprised that Tom remembered me. It felt good to meet this old friend and to recall our basketball glory days.

The following day, I attended the Celebration of Life Mass at the Jesuit parish St. Ignatius, where Dorothea and Mary Anne had been parishioners for a long time. After Mass there was a reception at the firehouse up the street.

The firehouse was filled with former colleagues from Notre Dame Prep, family and friends. Also in attendance were co-workers from Blue Cross Blue Shield, where Mary Anne was well respected and had spent years in a high-ranking position. I chose a table with friends and teachers from my high school.

A middle-aged woman, walking with a slight waddle, approached our table. Shoulder-length brown hair surrounded her somewhat puffy, round face.

"Pam?" she said, addressing me directly. "I am Rosemary, Dorothea's younger sister."

"When Dorothea was eighteen, her father died leaving Dorothea's mom with three teenagers, Dorothea, Val and Ricky. She remarried Jim, a long-time neighbor, and I was born a few years later. There's a 20-year age difference between me and Dorothea. I am also a

21

teacher, but I didn't start teaching until after I had children. I teach high school math in a public school in Florida. I got divorced last year, and the kids, Logan, Courtney and Megan, all teenagers, live with me."

Curious as to why this person had so extensively introduced herself to me with an abbreviated bio, I was a little apprehensive, but also wondering what would come next.

"I heard that Dorothea and Mary Anne taught you in high school. I wanted to talk to you in private, if you don't mind."

I excused myself from my group of friends and went with Rosemary to a corner of the firehouse.

"Well, my dear, what can you tell me about Mary Anne and my sister Dorothea?"

Her question and the way she addressed me as "my dear" were unsettling. Somehow, she thought I possessed some sort of insider information that could be of use to her. Who was this woman who had picked me out of a group to ask me what I knew about her sister and her friend? I needed to decide if it was simply sibling rivalry dirt she wanted or something more. But, why me? I surmised I would have to carefully word what I said to her.

Still uneasy about her query, I said: "I knew Dorothea and Mary Anne as teachers in my high school. As a junior I was in Dorothea's U.S. history class. I always considered her to be one of best, most fair and unbiased teachers at the school. Dorothea still remembers how I tried to get her off topic at the beginning of each class. I also remember Mary Anne as a compassionate, organized homeroom teacher, and faithful supporter of the schools' basketball games."

Impatient and unsatisfied with my answer, Rosemary added, "No, what was Dorothea like in the classroom, did they like her? Do you think she is a nice person? What do people think of her?" Perplexed by the line of questions, I replied, "I don't know, I liked her."

Her direct questions startled me. Did she want me to describe Dorothea's character? As her sister, she must have known Dorothea's character. Why would she want to know what I or other people thought of her? I became increasingly aware that she was fishing for some dirt on her sister. I thought for a moment and replied, "I can tell you a couple stories from the classroom that I remember happening." Seemingly interested, Rosemary motioned for me to continue. "Well, there was the time Dorothea was talking about Peter Stuyvesant and describing his misfortune and ended the lesson by saying, 'he was on his last leg.'"

Rosemary stared at me, there was no response. Dead silence. Obviously not having any idea why this was a funny comment. "Peter Stuyvesant on his last leg. His nickname was Peg Leg Pete after one of his legs had been shattered by a cannonball," I explained. She looked perplexed and didn't seem to know what I was talking about, and didn't care. It wasn't what she was after. Okay, I figured I'd try again. "There was the time, one Monday morning she came into class visibly shaken." Rosemary seemed interested in this story. "AND?" "Well, she told the class about her big, white dog named Guilford, who was accidentally cut with the scissors when Mary Anne and Dorothea attempted to give Guilford a haircut… the white dog was bleeding, crying and tracking blood all over the place." The experience must have been very upsetting for them. At the time, as a 17-year-old with a large dog that my dad and I gave haircuts to, I could easily relate to the story and empathize with them. I was looking at Rosemary for acceptance of the story yet got a look of disappointment instead. "But that's all I've got."

This interaction is important to note, because Rosemary told police in 2019, that I claimed to be a former student, but she did so, in a manner that was misleading and meant to be interpreted negatively, as if it was not true. It is a truthful statement and in 2017, Rosemary knew I was actually a former student as I relayed personal information about Dorothea from the 1980's, to Rosemary, that she knew to be an actual event, with accurate descriptions and real names.

Deciding not to entertain her any longer, I excused myself and, without answering her last questions, returned to my friends. Noticing I was visibly agitated, a former teacher who was sitting at my table asked, "What was that all about?"

"That woman is weird," I blurted out. "Let's just say it was interesting and her questions were kind of creepy."

"I briefly talked to her a while ago," said the former teacher. "She seemed catty to me. She was making comments about all the work needed to get Dorothea out of her house and was rolling her eyes."

"I thought everyone in the family lived in Philadelphia, but Rosemary said she was from Florida. Is she staying with Dorothea and helping out?" I asked. The teacher just shrugged, "I don't know."

This first meeting with one of Dorothea's family members had been unnerving. A few days after the wake, despite my apprehension about my first meeting with one of Dorothea's family members, I sent a message to Rosemary: "Since I only live a few minutes away, I could check on your sister from time to time and let you know how she is doing." I never got a response.

A couple of weeks after the funeral, Dorothea and Mary Anne's family sent me a card: "Thank you for your ongoing support for Mary Anne. We are still in shock and really need your support. We appreciate it." A month later Dorothea sent me another note: "Thank you for your help and companionship. It means a lot."

Some weeks later I gave Dorothea a call. Her brother Ricky answered and said she would be back in fifteen minutes.

Dorothea called back. "My brother is leaving in a few days, and I would love to go out for lunch. You would have to pick me up because I still don't feel comfortable driving."

"Okay! No problem. How about at Michael's Cafe? It's a nice place and we can sit outside on the patio if the weather is good."

A few days later, we enjoyed a two-hour lunch on the patio at Michael's Cafe. Dorothea seemed relaxed.

I started off by recalling the day Dorothea lectured my class about Peter Stuyvesant, being on his last leg and explained to Dorothea that I had retold the story to Rosemary when she asked me how Dorothea was as a teacher. I mentioned that I was surprised when Rosemary didn't find it humorous. Dorothea remarked, "Of course she didn't get it. She is a math teacher and wouldn't get it."

Upon choosing the crab cake special from Michael's menu, Dorothea said, "This is my first outing since the funeral. I have been avoiding people for quite some time. But I have been reminiscing about all the good times Mary Anne and I had together over the years."

"Good for you, Dorothea. Recalling the good stuff is part of the healing process." Dorothea proceeded, "You know, Mary Anne and I had lived in a three-story house in the city for years. Our place was a favorite destination for the Notre Dame Prep faculty's Friday wine and cheese parties, which often expanded into dinner parties with signature dishes. Many faculty members remember how these parties cemented a spirit of camaraderie among them."

The remainder of our lunchtime was filled with an exchange of memories of Notre Dame, the colleagues in the History Department, the fights between administration and faculty over the school philosophy, and the horrible days when the school was attacked by outsiders and the press for what they were teaching. Dorothea also proudly reported on some of her students who had made a difference in the lives of others in society.

After lunch, having learned that I had dogs, Dorothea asked me inside her home to meet Rosy, her rescued Cocker Spaniel. She also gave me a tour of the house.

"Look at this place, Pam. It's a dream house. When Mary Anne moved up the ladder to an executive position at the Blue Cross/Blue Shield headquarters, we decided to move out of Baltimore City and into Baltimore County. We bought this house in Glen Arm."

She guided me through the kitchen, where we grabbed a cup of coffee and walked through the large living room with a fireplace, and a den surrounded with windows giving access to a wrap-around deck, the four bedrooms, and the sprawling property with trees and shrubs.

We returned to the living room, continuing the conversation with our coffees.

"Mary Anne loved this house," said Dorothea, glancing around as if she expected her to appear at any moment. "Without her, we would never have found it. She was the kind of person who took care of all our finances and kept records of everything. I am rather easygoing when it comes to money: give me an account that allows me to write some checks and withdraw some cash, and I am content. Mary Anne's mind seemed always to think in numbers. My mind tries to understand how people screwed up their societies throughout the ages."

"My only memories of Mary Anne are from the time she was my homeroom teacher and when she attended the school's basketball games with you and several other teachers. I always thought she was well organized," I said.

"There are so many nice memories connected to this house, Pam. The cookouts we enjoyed with friends, the parties with the Notre Dame Prep faculty, and the quiet moments we enjoyed together . . . "

She glanced again around the living room again. "Even during her long sickness, Mary Anne never complained and endured the chemotherapy silently. Sometimes, I saw tears in her eyes, but she tried to hide them, I guess in order not to upset me. We never discussed it."

Dorothea blew her nose to hide the tears that were welling up in her eyes. But the memories kept coming. Sharing them with me seemed to make her feel a little better.

"When we bought this house, it was Mary Anne who worked out the details and made sure that we were joint tenants. It was also Mary Anne who came up with the idea to build a house in Sunset Beach in 2006. After a golf outing with her company, she fell in love with the area. It was very remote back in the day. Initially, and for a few years, we owned a condominium in a development set to expand into custom-built, single-family homes right on Oyster Bay Golf Links. Mary Anne was an avid golfer and really excelled at it. I liked golfing but was rather an average player. One day she asked me, 'Why don't we build our own home in North Carolina where we can get away, relax on the beach and play some golf? Later, when we are both retired, we can move there and enjoy a perennial vacation.' And that is just what she did. Along with the architect, she planned the house on one of the greens, and she supervised its building. We had some wonderful times in Sunset Beach and shared the place with family and friends for years."

Her face became somber when she added, "What will I do now, Pam? How can I stay here in Glen Arm in this big house when I replay that terrible event in my head over and over? I see her constantly when I go from one room to another. I've always wanted to move to Sunset Beach. I tried to get Mary Anne to move immediately following my retirement, but she wanted/needed to be close to her doctors here, so here we remained. Now, planning a move seems so overwhelming without the help of Mary Anne. It's just going to take some time to think this through, I guess."

I did not know if Dorothea was expecting me to answer, but I had the feeling that she was trying to reach out, feeling so alone in the world now. My once self-assured teacher now seemed forlorn and depressed. A deep compassion was welling up in my gut.

"Look, Dorothea, I can't answer that for you. Whatever you decide, I can be there to help you with some of the practical stuff, and some of the physical stuff, that you may need help with. From experience I know that everybody in your situation needs a helping hand. I could be that helping hand if you want, it's up to you, totally your decision."

She stared at me for a moment. Shaking her head, she said, "I don't know, Pam. I hate to be dependent on people."

"You depended on Mary Anne, didn't you? Look, Dorothea, you would not be the first person I've helped in these kinds of situations. Let me tell you a story.[2] I had a friend who was on permanent disability a few years ago. When her parents died, she had no place to live, and I invited her to live with me in my house in Indiana. Then when I took a new job in Georgia, I allowed her to keep living in my house in Indiana until she moved to Tennessee to live with her sister. Because of the recession, my company was bought out and I moved back to Maryland, where I helped my friend find a mobile home. For years I helped her maintain her modest property and made sure she had groceries and paid her bills."

"Lucky friend! I have to confess, yes, I was dependent on Mary Anne all these years. I do realize that from now on I will have to take care

---

[2] This story is related in a letter written in 2019 by that friend, who wrote a notarized affidavit to testify that I would never take advantage of people or exploit them.

of many things I am not very familiar with. It might not be easy. I am pushing seventy-five."

There was a long pause. She let her eyes wander around the room, as if she was searching for what to say next. As I had seen several times, her head tilted to the left. Wriggling uncomfortably in her chair, she said, "For me, it is still very difficult to talk about that dreadful Sunday morning in May. I have never shared this with anyone, but here it goes."

"Every Sunday morning, we had coffee together and then got ready to attend Mass at St. Ignatius. That morning, Mary Anne went to take a bath, and forty-five minutes later I noticed that the water was still running. I knocked on the door, but there was no answer. I called out her name but again got no answer.

Having had a double mastectomy, Mary Anne was a 10-year breast cancer survivor, but the cancer had returned in the past year and this time had spread to her brain. She had survived the chemo treatments, but they had taken a serious toll on her physically. She had lost all her hair and although she was never a heavy person, she had gotten terribly thin, as the chemo had made her sick. She didn't have much of an appetite and that which she did eat, she could barely keep down. Even I lost a lot of weight during this time, neither of us were really making any effort to eat, at least not in the way we had done in the past, eating out. She seemed to be wasting away to nothing, it was so sad."

She took a deep breath before continuing. "I opened the bathroom door and saw Mary Anne lying flat out in the full tub, motionless. Only afterwards did I learn that she had had an aneurysm, then fallen face down into the tub and drowned, a sponge blocking the drain. I was not strong enough to pull her out of the tub. I called some neighbors, but there was no answer. I called 911 and Mary Anne's family. The volunteer fire department arrived, followed by the police."

Anger flashed across Dorothea's face. "The first responders placed her thin, naked, bald body near the front door for all to see. It was a horrible sight. It was very disrespectful, I thought."

"I understand that you were upset, Dorothea, but the responders were not intentionally disrespecting Mary Anne's body. They see so much distress on a daily basis that they sometimes forget how things can traumatize bystanders or family. I know this from my own experience as a police officer and a firefighter and . . . " She interrupted me: "What upset me most was that the emergency personnel told me that it was unclear if this was accidental or otherwise. What did they mean? Did they think I killed my lifelong friend? My next-door neighbor, a practicing criminal lawyer, assured me that such an idea was absurd, and she was ready to defend me if they continued this line of thought."

"I do understand how all of this traumatizes you and that you have a difficult time being in this house. You are replaying the events in your head and are reliving the images of Mary Anne in the tub and on the floor and the helplessness you felt."

"Do you really know how I feel, Pam? I lost my lifelong friend in a terrible accidental death. I cannot let go of the images of that morning."

Blowing her nose, she kept staring at the floor. "I feel lost and terribly alone," she mumbled.

For a while I was at a loss for words. I finally broke the silence. "Look, Dorothea, do not think you are the only one who has gone through a situation like this. I understand what it is to mourn. When I was twenty-two and teaching, I had a close friend who shared my passion for art. He inspired me to reach for new avenues in the arts and painting. And then my friend suddenly died a year after my college graduation. It threw my world into complete and utter turmoil. For months I was distraught and felt terribly alone, angry, and empty. Immersing myself totally in teaching did not help. It was only time that brought some relief. So, I

30

know the fog that grief can create, and I understand the depression that follows. You must hang in there, Dorothea. Hang in there; believe me, it does get better with time. Mary Anne is looking out for you. You've got a guardian angel sitting on your shoulder. You know that, right?"

A faint smile came over Dorothea's face. "I am beginning to feel that I might have two angels. Thank you for listening, Pam. I feel relieved telling you the story."

Then she hesitantly added, "Well, there is something you can do for me. Before you leave, could you have a look at my computer? Some things do not seem to work. I asked some of my neighbors for help, but I don't want to impose on them any further." I was happy to do it. The problem was easily fixable: whoever had set up her account had misspelled her last name.

The lunch and the house visit had been a blessing. Dorothea had been able to focus on the happy memories at the school and her life with Mary Anne. It was also the first time she had the courage to recall the awful details of Mary Anne's passing and share with somebody her fear for a future by herself.

The lunch and house visit gave me a glance into the depth of her sadness and her feelings of helplessness. I knew, more than ever, that she needed help, and I was determined not to let her experience the overwhelming depression that I had experienced after my friend died. Asking me to help her with a computer problem was the first sign she would be willing to accept my offer to help her.

Now, five years from reconnecting with Dorothea after Mary Anne's death, my detractors saw me as a threat and were accusing me of trying gain her trust to insert myself into Dorothea's life to be able to take advantage of her later, for my own financial gain.

31

I have always helped people who needed a hand: family, friends, neighbors, and even strangers. And I never helped them with the expectation of being rewarded, financially or otherwise. I hate anyone who takes advantage of other people, especially children, seniors, or the disabled. It was my compassion for Dorothea's situation that drove me to come to her aid. That is just who I am.

June 2017: The Family's First Move

I knew Dorothea's sister Rosemary only from the uncomfortable meeting during Mary Anne's wake. I was still wondering why she had picked me out of a crowd of people who also knew Dorothea and Mary Anne. Rosemary's probing for me to say negative things about Dorothea had put me on guard. And it had been unsettling that she never answered my offer to check on Dorothea for her.

I tried to set Rosemary's probing aside. After all, who has a perfect family? I wanted to believe that it was good for Dorothea to have a sister and other family members to support her.

In time I learned that Dorothea had accompanied her younger sister to various functions during her high school and college years. She had spent summers and important holidays with Rosemary and her parents in other states. For years, Dorothea's nephew, Michael, had been her "golden boy." She was proud to be his godmother and had been involved in his life for a long time. He spent many a summer visiting her in Baltimore City and Glen Arm. She and Mary Anne even took him, as well as Rosemary, on a trip to Europe.

But after he graduated from college the contact between Dorothea and her sister Rosemary, brother Ricky, and nephew Michael had become limited and rather sporadic. (Ricky had two adopted sons, Michael the eldest, and David.) Nevertheless, Dorothea kept sending gift checks to them on holidays and birthdays, merely continuing the tradition that she had started when they were children, as checks weren't given as a result of them being close and actively assisting, visiting or contacting her. They were absent, by their own choosing. Due to some trouble David got involved in when he was younger, Dorothea was instructed not to send David money. This act could have many varied reactions or be perceived differently by those involved, if they did not fully know who made the

33

request and why. Michael might say, she preferred him. David might ask why he wasn't treated equally, feeling jilted. This could easily morph into perceptions held by others, that were not in Dorotheas best interest.

Dorothea told me that, two months before Mary Anne died, she had invited the whole family to celebrate her seventy-fifth birthday and she had sent a check for several thousand dollars to Rosemary with the memo "travel." Although there are photos from the celebration that include Mary Anne and Mary Anne's family, no records were found indicating that Dorothea's family had taken her up on this invitation, but she had cashed Dorothea's check.

I observed that Dorothea welcomed the presence and the assistance of Rosemary and her family in the early weeks of her loneliness. Her emails seemed to indicate that she looked forward to their visits, although Rosemary's habit of postponing or canceling these visits disappointed her. One time, Dorothea commented in an email, "We got lots done." Whether or not Dorothea had input and decision-making power was questionable, as Dorothea routinely rearranged things to her liking, after Rosemary's visit. Dorothea did not like to confront, or challenge Rosemary; she would just quietly go behind and changed things to her liking, after Rosemary was gone.

It was only much later that I learned about other events that happened in the early days after Mary Anne's passing. Barely four weeks after Mary Anne's death, Rosemary took Dorothea to Dorothea's lawyer. What happened during that visit made me begin to suspect that Dorothea's family had ulterior motives in helping her.

After the wake and Mass for Mary Anne at St. Ignatius, Rosemary returned to her home in Florida. A week later she came back to Glen Arm. I can only imagine the conversation between the two before they went to the lawyer.

Often, problems occur whereby others must make appointments for the elderly, because it is their schedule which is impacted since they drive elders to their

appointments. But elders need to be included in these three-way calls, in order to be knowledgeable and can approve of the discussion at hand; so as not be left out, ignored or overruled.

It was only a few weeks after Mary Anne's sudden death, and Dorothea was still grieving and disoriented. She was foggy enough that she wasn't driving, because she recognized she couldn't concentrate. That being the case, was she clear enough to change her legal documents, in a manner that financially benefitted one person over another by 100%? Rosemary did drive her to a lawyer however, and Dorothea signed a Power of Attorney for Rosemary. But was this necessary, since Rosemary was already a secondary POA? We have to ask, why the rush? Dorothea also made changes to her will and later that same day, made beneficiary changes to her financial investment account, again benefiting one family member over another by 100%. Was she in the right state of mind to make these kinds of decisions at that meeting? Later, Dorothea would not remember what happened at the appointment with the lawyer. She never told me that legal documents had been drawn up at that meeting. I only became aware of it two years later, just before my arrest. *The document was never submitted nor certified by the courts until after my arrest.*

At the meeting, Dorothea removed her brother Ricky completely from her will and gave Rosemary his portion of the estate. Prior to this change, the will directed that Ricky and Rosemary would share one half of the estate while the other half was split between the three nephews and two nieces. Why Dorothea removed her brother from her will remains unknown. I did learn, however, that Dorothea deeply disliked Ricky's wife. They were not even on speaking terms.

During the same appointment, the lawyer drew up a limited Power of Attorney with Rosemary as the primary Power of Attorney and Dorothea's nephew Michael, as the successor POA. In an introductory statement, that document says that, although the heading says, "limited power of attorney," the principal intends to grant what was previously commonly referred to as a "general durable power of attorney." The agent's authority would continue until the principal died or revoked the power of attorney.[3]

In the POA document signed by Dorothea, she gives Rosemary practically full powers over all aspects of her possessions and investments, including the power to change beneficiaries, in case Dorothea was declared incapacitated. It is noteworthy to mention that at this time, and at no time earlier, did either Rosemary or Michael have joint accounts with Dorothea and, neither were POA's on Dorothea's bank accounts nor had authority to access Dorothea's bank accounts. Bank Signature Cards are the proof that neither name was on Dorothea's bank accounts. This was contrary to what Rosemary told the Fidelity Investment advisor in a phone call, in 2017.

In addition, Dorothea signed an advance health care directive that gave Rosemary and Michael full powers and authority to make health care decisions for Dorothea, including the power to place her in a nursing home or other facility. Dorothea never got a copy of that document. A "Do Not Resuscitate" directive was not included in the legal documents. Rosemary would add this legal directive after she gained full control of Dorothea in Florida courts.

Later that same day, a change was made to Dorothea's considerable Fidelity Investments account: her brother Ricky was eliminated as beneficiary and replaced by Rosemary.

---

[3] The document sent to my attorneys was missing the seal of the notary who signed it. Furthermore, the copy of that POA was not certified by Baltimore County Circuit Court until June 27, 2019, seven days after my arrest. It was then used by Rosemary to petition for her guardianship over Dorothea in July 2019. It was not certified in North Carolina courts until May of 2021.

In hindsight, Dorothea's decision to give Rosemary Power of Attorney was the first step along the path that would lead to Rosemary having complete control over Dorothea's life and assets. One must bear in mind that this power of attorney becomes effective only when the grantor is declared unable to make rational decisions

because of mental or physical incapacity. There was no indication that Dorothea was incapacitated in 2017. She was traumatized by finding her friend dead, feeling as if she had failed to help her friend; she was overwhelmed with the decisions people were asking her to make, as she was grieving and in a fog. All of these things are normal, understandable and temporary. But the stage was set, and two years later the family would do everything to prove Dorothea's incapacity and obtain full guardianship.

I find it very sad, that Dorothea's lawyer revised documents in a way that significantly changed the financial outcome of the beneficiaries, while the elder was significantly compromised due to a documented traumatic event, and temporarily placed on medication for depression within the same time frame. Given how the financial changes significantly benefitted one family member, at the expense of another is a questionable action, but aligning that financial set up, with changing the dynamics of a POA, giving that same benefactor, control over Dorothea's financial and medical welfare, should have red flags all over it. The changes doubled Rosemary's inheritance, made her the beneficiary of Dorothea's Fidelity Investments account, and gave Rosemary Power of Attorney. It reeks of premeditation, but it only gets worse.

At some point, Dorothea had told me that Rosemary had divorced her husband because he was too controlling. Is this what Rosemary was telling others? In fact, court documents show that her husband filed for divorce and finalized it in 2016, a few months prior to Mary Anne's death. As a settlement, Rosemary would get several thousand dollars a month for four years.

Were Rosemary's maneuvers aimed at making sure that her sister became a source of income when the divorce payments ended? Rosemary was not included in Mary Anne's will and believed that Dorothea was now the owner of two properties and considerable other assets. Did she believe that Dorothea and Mary Anne were a couple, life partners, and expected Dorothea to inherit the majority

of Mary Anne's estate? Was this what motivated her to get half of Dorothea's estate and half of her investments at the 2017 meeting? Was this why she thought I had stolen large amounts of money? Was this why she wanted Dorothea under guardianship? We will never know, and I can only speculate, but it is important to raise the questions. In the police report, Rosemary states that her sister had a life partner of 40 years. Rosemary also stated in a Department of Social Services report that Dorothea was an alcoholic. Dorothea not only told me that her sister would lie to get what she wanted, Dorothea also told police in 2019, as it was recorded on body cam footage.

Two days after these legal and financial meetings took place, Rosemary drove Dorothea and her dog to Dorothea's summer home in Sunset Beach. In statements made to police in 2019, Rosemary states that this was Dorothea's permanent move to North Carolina.

A week later Rosemary returned to Florida, leaving Dorothea alone in her Sunset Beach home. Rosemary knew that Dorothea was now alone in North Carolina, yet with a fully loaded, unsecured house in Glen Arm, Maryland. She knew Dorothea did not have a primary care physician, dentist, hair stylist, or podiatrist in North Carolina. The bulk of Dorothea's clothes were still in Glen Arm; and her mail was not being forwarded, and there wasn't a single account that had been updated with "a supposedly new permanent address." There were no safety or security measures in place for a person who would live there all by herself. She would have to rely on some friends and friendly neighbors to get through the coming days and months. Is it possible that Dorothea was being set up to fail?

Is it possible that Rosemary, knowing that Dorothea was depressed, and grieving, anticipated Dorothea to rely on alcohol in an attempt to feel less pain? Was it possible that Rosemary expected Dorothea to drink to excess, subsequently fall, hurting herself to such an extent, that by being alone, would make it nearly impossible for anyone to come to Dorothea's aid in the nick of time? Did Rosemary

foresee Dorothea pass, one way or another, by her own undoing? It's quite obvious that the stage was set for Rosemary to benefit from such an event, and claim no knowledge. There was no safety net for Dorothea.

Because of my own experience of a friend dying, I kept in touch with Dorothea every couple of days by phone or email just to make sure she was doing well.

A Year of Apartment Living

After two weeks of being alone in Sunset Beach, Dorothea invited me to visit, and I accepted. She seemed excited to know she would have a friend visit. She told Rosemary that I would be visiting Sunset Beach. Suddenly, Rosemary promised to visit her on June 23. Dorothea called to tell me to postpone the trip because Rosemary was returning to visit. I didn't think anything of it. I was just glad that Dorothea wasn't going to be alone. However, almost as soon as Dorothea conveyed the update, Rosemary turned around and told Dorothea she couldn't make the trip after all. So, Dorothea extended another invitation to me. This time we planned on the July 4th weekend. Sure enough, as soon as she told Rosemary her plans, Rosemary tells Dorothea that won't work because she is traveling to Sunset Beach for the same weekend. Dorothea then calls me to say we have to cancel the plans again. I didn't know it at the time, but this actually became a pattern with Rosemary. This is typical behavior of "gaslighting." I was unfamiliar with it at the time. I just felt sorry for Dorothea bouncing around like a ping pong ball. I assured Dorothea everything was okay and if she ever needed a friend, I was there for her.

In mid-July, Dorothea received an email from Mary Anne's brother telling the family that Mary Anne's interment was scheduled for early August. Dorothea called Rosemary asking her to drive her back home to attend the ceremony, but Rosemary refused. She refused to make any kind of travel arrangements for Dorothea. Dorothea called me, saying, "I asked Rosemary for help, but she refused. I told her I was going to ask you, and she is against that, but I don't have a Plan A. Can you be my Plan B?" I wholeheartedly agreed to help. We arranged for her to rent a car for me, where I would drive down in the rental, drop it off in Shallotte, NC and then I would drive her and her dog back to Maryland in her SUV.

It was my first visit to the Sunset Beach property. The house Mary Anne had planned and built was remarkably beautiful. It had a view of the green and a lake from a large back deck. There were high ceilings and hardwood flooring, three bedrooms and three and a half baths, a double garage, lots of light throughout the house, a well-appointed kitchen with a separate dining room. It was an ideal summer home.

During my visit, I observed Dorothea in her daily routines. She liked Waterford crystal, wall hangings, strong coffee, walks, wildlife, the ocean, and eating out. She enjoyed watching the news, *Jeopardy!* and *Wheel of Fortune* and was most relaxed when she was watching the beautiful views and sunsets from her back deck. She was also often on her computer reading emails or Facebook posts.

That first weekend in North Carolina, I also noticed how much Chardonnay Dorothea was drinking. I'm not a wine drinker, and she could easily drink me under the table. I would later learn that she would drink more when she was upset. Her habit would later become a worrisome subject we discussed, and she admitted that she and Mary Anne had discussed it previously. Years earlier they had backed off the hard liquor and moved to wine, exclusively. She felt that change had been enough of an improvement. She said she never drove if she drank. If she was away from home, she always arranged for a designated driver.

During this first visit to Sunset Beach, I got to know Dorothea's new community. She directed me through town, driving to the area's sights and shops, and I met some of the neighbors who had become close to her. It was obvious that Dorothea loved Sunset Beach and the house. She told me what an ideal place it was for her to retire. Her signature statement was, "Who wouldn't love this place?"

I arrived in North Carolina on the 28th and we returned to Maryland on the 30th. We walked through her home, to make sure it was safe, and it was. Mary Anne's family had been checking on the house while Dorothea was away. Not much had changed; it still felt like home to

Dorothea, as 90% of the house remained intact. Only a few anticipated belongings of Mary Anne's had been removed by her family.

After the funeral, Dorothea stayed at the Glen Arm house rather than returning to North Carolina. After talking to friends and neighbors, she decided to begin the process of getting the house ready for sale, and plan her move to the summer home in North Carolina. Once again, that which Rosemary told the police in 2019 of Dorothea having made a permanent move to North Carolina in June was fabricated.

Dorothea told Rosemary of her plans and immediately Rosemary contacted realtors and scheduled them to meet with Dorothea. However, Dorothea didn't like how they treated her, so she called and hired an agent who lived a few houses away from her in her Glen Arm neighborhood. It was time to pack up, clean up and prepare the house to go on the market.

I was tasked with accomplishing the items on the agent's to-do list. I spent all my free time helping Dorothea ready her home: power washing the exterior, stripping wallpaper and prepping the walls for the painters, hiring electricians, boxing items to move to North Carolina, and taking items to Goodwill or the landfill. I had sold a couple of my own houses, and that experience came in handy.

Make no mistake, Dorothea made all the decisions and approved the costs involved in updating the property. I did the research and the physical work. I never requested any kind of payment and Dorothea never offered. We were friends, and that's what friends do, they help each other out, period. While the house was shaping up, I drove her to her exercise facility, where she had a group of friends she met each time. I took her to the doctor, to the bank, to the grocery store, and to her investment broker. Dorothea asked me to drive her to St. Ignatius on Sundays. This became a weekly routine, and a social outlet for Dorothea.

Some people thought this was really odd, spending so much time with an older person, but it had been a long-standing routine of mine for as long as I could remember. I had always done these things for my aunts until they passed. Then my dad got ill and I helped Mom care for him. He had Alzheimer's, and it was a difficult as well as an exhausting time. In August of 2016, he passed. As many know, you give up everything to care for a loved one with Alzheimer's, and it takes a few months to decompress and get back to a normal life. During the time you are caring for them, you lose many friends, and become isolated due to the focus placed on your loved one. Now it was a year after his death, and I was healthy and able to care for someone else who needed a little extra help. For me, it was not unusual at all.

While all the activity centered on her home was going on, Dorothea began to be nostalgic about leaving the Glen Arm house she had shared with Mary Anne for so long. Though nostalgic, Dorothea was not as consumed with grief as she had been. She had slowly returned to some of her routines: going to the health center, visiting friends and neighbors, and meeting students and former co-workers at Notre Dame Prep.

She kept in touch with Mary Anne's brother, who was the executor of Mary Anne's estate, and recognized that it might take a year to close it out. So, before the movers gathered up items to be taken to North Carolina, Dorothea decided to remain in Baltimore County for one year, renting an apartment until Mary Anne's estate was finalized.

People maneuver through the grieving process differently. There is nothing wrong with changing plans, as people do it all the time. I still don't understand why Rosemary thought it was necessary for Dorothea to immediately move to North Carolina, since it wasn't Rosemary's decision to make. Rosemary remained in Florida.

At the end of August, I helped her look for apartments. She settled on a two-bedroom apartment in a gated community in Towson. The apartment was a ground level with a patio, which was great for the dog, and she could safely sit outside and enjoy the sun and greenery. It was quiet, yet close to shops and banks with off-street parking provided. She had chosen a two-bedroom apartment so that out-of-town family members would have a place to stay if they visited. Having furnished the apartment with items she had decided not to transport to North Carolina, she moved into the apartment in mid-October. It was the perfect transition place for her.

Time and again, Dorothea's family claimed that I promised to live with her in the apartment. Although Dorothea would occasionally allude to this regarding North Carolina, I told her that I would never do this. My mother was in her nineties and needed me on a daily basis. She was my priority. The problem with Rosemary's claims has multiple unresolved issues from top to bottom. Dorothea had a dog that was not social with other dogs. So much so that, a well-known, popular, professional dog whisperer, had met the dog, and concluded, "Rosy is in her own world; just turn her around to face a wall, when there is a second dog in the picture." I had two big dogs and Rosy did not get along with them. Also, the apartment had a limit on the number of pets, a resident could own, and a size limit on them. My dogs exceeded the set limitations. There are two more problems with Rosemary's claim. I cared for my mother in my mother's home. In addition to other routine things, I was her security force at night. The idea that I would place my mother at risk is unnerving. The last problem with Rosemary's claim is the idea that I would move from a 1400 square-foot split level, single-family home with a basement and yard, into a 750 square-foot apartment is outright laughable. Rosemary had a wild imagination, in the face of unrealistic possibilities, and yet made verifiably false statements, that authorities believed without a full and unbiased investigation.

By the end of October, Dorothea's house was on the market at an asking price of more than $520,000. One open house and she had immediate offers, one of which was accepted and eventually settled upon before the end of November. Dorothea wrote me: "I don't know how I could do this without you." I was happy for Dorothea. Retirement is not cheap, and never goes down in price. For me, it was instant gratification for all the work I did to help increase the selling price. The realtor was able to increase the initial asking price in Dorothea's contract by $20K.

Dorothea adjusted well to apartment living and felt quite comfortable in her new surroundings. Except for some problems with her dog Rosy, who usually pooped somewhere in the apartment, she was excited to live there. She knew the area well and could shop and bank nearby, meet friends and former colleagues, attend the church she had been going to for years, and continue to attend various functions held at the Notre Dame Prep, just around the corner.

Since Dorothea remained close by in Towson, I could continue to visit her when needed. I also kept in touch with her via emails and phone calls. Her Glen Arm house was sold, and all she had to do was to prepare to ultimately move to her retirement home in Sunset Beach.

The biggest challenge for Dorothea was getting used to living by herself after several decades of sharing her life with Mary Anne. She had to take care of many things that Mary Anne had been responsible for all those years and that Dorothea, in a sense, had taken for granted. Living alone in an apartment for a year would give her time to prepare for living alone at her home in North Carolina.

Dorothea needed to get used to providing for daily necessities and taking care of monthly bills. Mary Anne had been the financial guru who kept detailed documentation on everything, from doctors' reports to stock investments, usually with notes and questions scribbled on them. Dorothea, on the other hand, was a document minimalist: documents came in, she glanced at them, and then she threw them away. With Mary Anne gone, Dorothea knew she had to change her approach. Together we accessed her accounts, and I showed her how to set up auto payments. It took time to convince her to keep recent billings and review them online, but she ultimately agreed to do it.

Dorothea had regular contact with her financial advisor at Fidelity Investments. I drove her to the appointments which she had arranged. At the first meeting, he asked me to remain in the lobby. I didn't think anything odd about that. I didn't have any intention of sitting in on someone's financial review. My parents had always been very private in this manner, and it carried over to my way of thinking about personal finances. Her relationship with her financial advisor was very candid. He confronted Dorothea regarding a phone call he had received from her sister Rosemary. Once again, Rosemary concocted an unsupported story accusing me of attempted wrong-doing with Dorothea's bank accounts. Upon hearing it, Dorothea denied it happened and insisted that I sit in at the meetings as a second set of ears, so if she had a question later, I might know the answer. He came out to the lobby and to my surprise, invited me to join their meeting. Once seated, he revealed that Rosemary had been in contact with him because she was concerned about my involvement with Dorothea. She accused me of entering a bank, requesting to remove her name from Dorothea's accounts and add my name to the accounts, and had advised him to be very cautious. I was dumbfounded. Why would she make up such a story? How would I defend myself from such an accusation? This cemented my red flag on anything Rosemary said or touched. I was grateful that the financial advisor brought this to the attention of both Dorothea and me. At this point, Rosemary revealed herself to be a devil without any disguise. I had to remain vigilant and on my toes. I had to document and keep everything; at every turn I had to cover my ass, I didn't know what she would try to do, or what stories she would tell, or to whom. It wasn't until I was reviewing the security video in 2019 (two years later), that I learned that Rosemary was never on Dorothea's bank accounts, as I heard her tell Dorothea, "You need to put me on your bank accounts." The security video provided me with the evidence I needed to prove her story to the financial advisor as a big fat lie. I would need to download and save the video, all in due time.

I accompanied Dorothea to many of these meetings, at her request. She enjoyed reviewing her investments, getting advice and making decisions. I made no decisions and had no input. On Dorothea's behalf, I gathered any information that the advisor requested, such as monthly expenses and income and expenditures data. He then reviewed and discussed plans with Dorothea.

Attending these meetings taught me a great deal about financial matters. It led to regular discussions about the stock market with Dorothea. At the age of fifty-six I had never felt the need for a financial advisor. I had meager savings and had moved in with my parents in 2010 to help my mother care for my father, who had Alzheimer's and subsequently died in 2016. I was living on the modest salary I earned as a fire safety inspector. I visited schools, childcare facilities, foster families and families seeking to adopt. I was tasked in making sure the required annual testing by certified technicians had been done in keeping with national standards, and local codes. I also looked for, and educated families about other fire life safety issues that might impede egress in the event of an emergency.

When it came to financial matters, I was like a sponge in the meetings, eagerly absorbing all the information I could from Dorothea's financial advisor. So, in the event I stumbled across something that I should know about, or that could benefit Dorothea, I would know how to advise her. The new information I learned could possibly even be applied to my meager finances.

Rosemary and Michael made me out to be maliciously involved in Dorothea's financial matters. If making sure her bills were paid and questioning why there was a large amount of money magically appearing and disappearing each month in a lump sum in her investment statements, and bringing it to the attention of her finance people is being maliciously

47

involved in financial matters, our society is doomed by the lurking vultures. One thing is certain, Rosemary was good at getting people to believe dirt on others, when dirt didn't exist. I never did anything without first discussing it with Dorothea or asking for her input. She was the homeowner and the person of record in all her financial matters. She made all the decisions but needed help to carry out her decisions. It never crossed my mind that I was mirroring Mary Anne, until a neighbor in North Carolina mentioned, "You do everything Mary Anne did, just quicker...well, because you're younger."

Some have suggested I could have saved myself a lot of trouble had I asked Dorothea to state in writing that I was to help with her financial matters. But that would not have been enough. The family even claimed that I signed, or I had Dorothea sign checks, for my benefit. Again, these were all untrue and without documentation to prove the accusations. They could have gone so far as to suggest any planned document was coerced. I would not suggest as others have, that a single signed document is enough to keep the vultures at bay. In the past, as someone who just stepped up to help without hesitation, helping never required a waiver, or contingency or a bill of health or a video of proof of mental capacity. It was a selfless act of generosity, and the only return I could have expected was a "thank you" or a smile. Family vultures and greed within the court system, among lawyers, doctors, and social services "professionals" are lying in wait, just clamoring for a chance to swoop down and to catch easy prey. It's imperative, that you protect yourself from them. Stay one step ahead of them by being honest at all cost. Don't let your guard down.

Between August 2017 and November 2018, I drove Dorothea to her home in North Carolina and back, at least once a month, usually over long weekends. Prior to each trip, I made sure that my mother had easy to fix dinners, groceries and any other necessities for these weekends. Neighbors were made aware that she was alone, good neighbors who were ready to help her if she needed them.

My truck was always packed with specifically chosen, and sometime more fragile, home furnishings that Dorothea had not entrusted the movers to take, but wanted transported to Sunset Beach. Every trip down was a working weekend: doing home maintenance, unpacking boxes from the movers, making small repairs, and doing yard work.

In June 2017 Rosemary had packed boxes with some items she wanted for herself and her children, and put stickers on some of the furniture she wanted Dorothea to move to North Carolina. Rosemary said she planned to pick these things up later in North Carolina and bring them all to Florida. It should be noted here that Rosemary, after her July 2017 visit, did not make any further effort to see Dorothea until July 2018, when Dorothea traveled to Florida.

If you want to be specific, phone records show that Rosemary stopped contacting Dorothea in the fall of 2017 after Dorothea sold her house. With the exception of Rosemary telling Dorothea, she and her girls planned a brief visit over the Christmas holiday vacation, this was followed by a phone call after the holidays telling Dorothea time got away from them. All other phone calls to Dorothea didn't resume until February 2018. One could make the case that Rosemary took away family updates from Dorothea, and removed and isolated Dorothea from knowing what her nieces and nephews were up to, something that Rosemary previously provided to Dorothea. Was it because Dorothea moved into an apartment against Rosemary's advice? We don't know, but it seems likely. It follows the pattern of someone "gaslighting" an elderly person. If someone is withholding a form of love, which is inclusion in family happenings, it has intentional psychological effects. Dorothea sought to be included in family events and was hurt when she learned she was excluded.

When Rosemary canceled their holiday visit again in 2018, I felt horrible for Dorothea, it would be another holiday alone for her. I knew my brother and his wife would be staying with my mom, so I arranged to celebrate the holidays with Dorothea instead of with my family. During that Christmas vacation, Dorothea handed me a check for $5,000 with "Happy Holidays" written on the memo line. I objected that there were too many zeros on the check, but she said that I was her "angel" and that she "never could have done what she did without me." It was her way of thanking me for what I had done for her in the past year and a half. Unfortunately, her generous Christmas check would also be used against me, and factor into the charges of financial abuse.

With the exception of the initial contact with a real estate agent, neither Rosemary nor Dorothea's brother Ricky were involved in any part of the decision making, repairs, cleaning, packing, documentation, renovation, and the staging of the Glen Arm property, although they repeatedly claimed otherwise. Ricky even claimed he physically drove her to North Carolina to help her move. One of the real estate agents later testified that Dorothea never mentioned Rosemary assisting her during the selling process.

After establishing her position as Dorothea's POA soon after Mary Anne's death, Rosemary (and her family) practically disappeared from the scene. Why did they not offer their help in selling her Glen Arm house? Why did they not visit her in her new apartment to see how she was adjusting? After all, Dorothea had chosen a two-bedroom apartment so there would be room for them to stay. Did Dorothea ask herself these questions? I wondered, but I never asked her.

All in all, Dorothea's apartment stay went relatively well for a number of months. She continued to visit the University Health Club, occasionally went to restaurants, attended Sunday Mass at St. Ignatius, and kept in contact with former colleagues and friends.

I was visiting one day when the postman delivered a good-sized box. It was 15" wide, 18" long 4" deep. "Ooh, what did you get?" I was curious, and she seemed nonplussed as she opened the box. I scrunched up my face, as I peered into the box. "A back brace? You have a bad

50

back?" "No, but it was free". "What?" I soon found out that she was prone to be taken in by "phone scammers" that prey on elderly people who live alone. She would sometimes give out her credit card information to donate to charities without researching if they were legitimate. I now had a new task. I had to educate her about never donating over the phone or giving personal information to callers. She was unaware that Medicare never asks anyone for personal information over the phone. The following month I showed her where her free back brace had actually been billed against her Medicare. However, it wasn't soon enough as yet another medical device arrived at her door. This time however, the postman was nice enough to realize what was going on and immediately took it back and returned it to the sender.

In 2018, while helping her to gather tax information for her accountant, we learned that charities were putting unauthorized monthly charges on her credit cards. I canceled those charges on her behalf, and I asked Dorothea to choose a handful of charities she cared about and usually donated to. Both Mary Anne and Dorothea had always shown an abiding, deep empathy for the less fortunate. They kept a long list of charities that were receiving their generous donations. They gifted anonymously to fund drives and handed money to homeless people they passed along the street on their way to church.

A few months later, she learned about Fidelity Investments' Charity Fund, I researched her giving history and identified the nonprofits with high ratings. With the assistance of her financial advisor, I helped her set up and distribute to her charities via Fidelity Investments in a manner that was consistent with her history of giving and was easily traceable for tax purposes. Her charitable giving averaged about $10,000 a year to schools, colleges, veterans organizations, St. Jude's, the Sierra Club, and others. On her own level, she was as charitable as Mary Anne, who supported a range of organizations. Dorothea routinely followed Mary Anne's lead.

In mid-June 2018, Dorothea tripped over her dog and fell. The fall knocked her unconscious. In an email to me she wrote: "Fell hard and knocked myself out. Fell hard and there was blood on the floor. Got to bed by twelve." I rushed over and took her to the emergency room, where she got four stitches in her head.

I became worried when she complained that she was sometimes "foggy and unsteady." I relayed that to her doctors at a local hospital. The tests revealed that she had a vitamin B12 deficiency. Some symptoms of that deficiency are anemia, lack of balance and coordination, dizziness, and often, forgetfulness. I had noticed that Dorothea was sometimes repeating herself, asking the same question twice and then correcting herself with an "Oh, yes, you just told me that!" With a series of monthly B12 shots, her doctor brought her back to normal B12 levels and the symptoms disappeared.

On more than one occasion, I noticed that she was slurring her speech on the phone. I also knew she had a pattern to start drinking wine early in the day when she was upset or felt lonely. I also noticed that she was not eating enough. Some honest emails and a couple of sit-downs were needed to make her aware that she had to take better care of herself. I knew that being alone in North Carolina would be difficult for her, and we talked about it. She assured me she would be okay.

In late June 2018, Rosemary invited Dorothea to visit her and her children in Florida. I worked with Rosemary on arranging the flights to and from Florida. Unbeknownst to Dorothea, her sister had also invited her brother Ricky. For some reason, the relationship between Dorothea and Ricky had been tenuous for some time. It is still unclear why Dorothea removed Ricky from her will in 2017.

From Florida, Dorothea called me and told me Ricky and Rosemary planned outings that she was not interested in; so she remained in the house for the better part of two weeks. Her Florida visit became dreadful, with the exception of spending time with Rosemary's dog, which Dorothea enjoyed.

In a number of text messages before the Florida visit, Rosemary had insisted she thought that Dorothea had Alzheimer's. I kept telling her that a diagnosed B12 deficiency was causing Dorothea's memory issues. I had taken care of my father, who had Alzheimer's, and knew that Dorothea's problems were very different and were manageable. Spelling errors in emails, grief after losing a lifelong friend, slurred speech, and fogginess are not the kinds of Alzheimer's symptoms I had witnessed in my father. Dorothea's issues were the result of her B12 deficiency, her drinking habits, or her lack of proper nutrition. Rosemary, however, kept insisting that Dorothea was suffering from dementia. Did Rosemary and Ricky get together in Florida to evaluate and plan a take-over of Dorothea? Did Ricky know that Rosemary had assisted in completely removing him from Dorothea's will, and as a beneficiary in her financial investments? Did Rosemary tell him that she was to get his share of Dorothea's estate? I doubt it. Either way, it was a no-win situation for Ricky. If he knew she had removed him completely, would he be seen as retaliating? If he didn't know she had removed him, then he would be viewed as a co-conspirator in Rosemary's grand plan. His best option was to tell the truth, but he didn't. His statements to police and to the Florida courts are documented proof that he lied.

Rosemary told me early on that Dorothea was "mean and nasty." When I told Rosemary that Dorothea had never been mean and nasty to me, she shot back, "Maybe she thinks you're her last hope." And I replied, "I don't know, but maybe I am." Was Rosemary the best suited person to lookout for Dorothea's best interests? Rosemary's statement was repeated to the Department of Social Services in June 2019, but I didn't learn of her statements to the Department of Social Services until February of 2022.

Perhaps Rosemary did not know her sister as well as she thought she did. Dorothea indeed had some issues with social interaction. Rosemary saw them as results of her advancing age or the onset of dementia instead of elements of Dorothea's character.

Over time, I observed some of Dorothea's character traits. One of Dorothea's issues was social interaction with other people. In a conversation she always seemed to be two steps ahead of you. You get the impression that she was not interested in what you were saying and had stopped listening. If she lost interest in what you were saying, she abruptly shut the whole topic down. She had a knack for inserting a totally off-the-wall comment that had nothing to do with the conversation at hand. Yet two weeks later she'd bring up the topic and inquire about your involvement and have remembered all the details you had spoken about.

In social situations, she would suddenly wander off without saying a thing. She was not interested in small talk and had a hard time identifying what interested others. What she herself found entertaining, funny, or sarcastic, others sometimes saw as odd. She had problems with eye contact and had trouble picking up on non-verbal cues during a conversation.

It was hard for her to participate in group activities; she tended not to speak to people with whom she felt uncomfortable. Changing a routine was distressing, and new situations were frightening for her. Her language was often defensive and sprinkled with dry sarcasm and teasing. While engaged in a conversation, she often seemed to respond in a manner to entertain herself, in an effort to gain a reaction from the person with whom she was speaking. It was rather a twisted form of personal entertainment, of which only she was aware. I found it humorous to observe. However, if you were the butt of her entertainment, you may think she was being nasty. This may have been one of the reasons why we got along.

On more than one occasion Dorothea arrived at a dinner party early, then wanted to leave before dinner was served. Dorothea's detractors have cited these character traits as signs of the onset of dementia. But actually, they are just a part of who Dorothea was.

One day she confided in me that as a youngster she was very self-conscious and put on a tough exterior to hide the hurt she felt when people were talking about her or did not include her in their activities. Her self-consciousness can be seen today in the shy, timid tilt of her head. Yet otherwise, she is a defensive, confident person.

I do believe that Mary Anne understood Dorothea well and was aware of the foibles of her character. She acted as her big sister, even though she was younger than Dorothea. Mary Anne accepted Dorothea as she was, which might be one of the reasons why they were longtime friends, and their friendship might have helped bridge gaps between Dorothea and other people.

In early fall 2018, I noticed Dorothea was asking me to drive more often. I questioned her on this, and she admitted she felt that her Honda SUV had become too big for her; subsequently, she had been driving less and less. At the suggestion of her financial advisor, I did some research on compact cars that she might find easier to drive. We went to several dealerships to look at cars. When we went to CarMax, she was able to sit in and compare many makes and models right on the spot. We were able to cross off many that just didn't suit her needs or likes. She chose a blue Chevy Spark ACTIV, which had to be shipped from Florida to North Carolina. After she moved out of her apartment, and settled into her summer home in North Carolina, she signed a note giving me permission to sell the Honda SUV on her behalf. She also asked if the car could remain in Maryland, parked in front of my house until a buyer could be located. She had hoped to help a needy family get a solid car. However, many didn't want to purchase at her asking price without a warranty. She even had work done and an inspection completed to help potential buyers consider the SUV. In the end, to get her asking price, I sold the Honda to CarMax on March 30, 2019 and deposited the check into Dorothea's bank account two days later, on April 1 at 3:30 P.M. But once again in 2019, even the new car purchase and the sale of the Honda SUV would become part of the family's charges against me. As they claimed that they should have been told about the sale of the SUV and the purchase of the car. Additionally, they claimed I stole the money from the sale of the SUV.

Dorothea was competent, engaged with the neighborhood community, had sold a home, signed a rental lease, successfully accomplished moving to another state, all without their involvement; yet, they claimed to police that Dorothea should have been keeping them informed of her every move, as if she required their approval. They failed to provide the bank statements that proved the CarMax check had been deposited and no money was missing.

Looking back at my many months of helping Dorothea, filled me with a sense of accomplishment. She enjoyed her apartment living and the social interaction with friends and colleagues; her medical and financial needs were set up properly; her charities were in safe hands; she got a car that was more suited to her needs; her house in Glen Arm was sold; and the weekend trips to Sunset Beach increased her desire to move there permanently.

Dorothea was still an older person who had lost a lifelong companion. What elderly person who loses a lifelong companion is not prone to extended grieving or periods of loneliness, leading to lack of self-care or changed eating habits? What senior is not at risk of falling or becoming more forgetful?

Dorothea might be a complicated person, but her year of apartment living had shown that she was able to make rational decisions about her own welfare. She had proven that she was capable of living by herself.

I had succeeded in making Dorothea's life better. She felt good about her decisions, and all of this had been done on her terms, and on her timeline.

November 2018: Sunset Beach for Good

Dorothea's apartment lease was coming to an end and she planned to move to Sunset Beach permanently in late November 2018. On several occasions she told me that she was ready and looking forward to that move. I was confident that the year of living by herself in an apartment had helped prepare her to live alone in North Carolina.

Dorothea had little contact with Mary Anne's family after Mary Anne's estate was settled. She would sometimes meet Mary Anne's brother, Lenny, and his wife at St. Ignatius church. She attended the groundbreaking when a local Catholic high school was the recipient of a large donation from the estate to upgrade the playing fields. The last time she interacted with Mary Anne's family was to celebrate Thanksgiving at Lenny's home in 2019. Lenny later mentioned that the prospect of finally moving to her summer home put her in a good mood.

Her unwanted furniture was donated, and although each month for the past year we had made trips to North Carolina, my truck was fully packed for the journey, as well. In anticipation of the move, I had arranged the transfer of her medications to North Carolina pharmacies, informed Social Security of her new address, and enrolled her in North Carolina Medicare.

Soon after the move, we discussed how she could make her big house as safe as possible. A security system could give her some peace of mind; someone could be notified if trouble occurred. She had good and reliable neighbors and a neighborhood association, but no further security. It was a quiet neighborhood, with limited street lighting, made up of mostly fellow retirees. Many of the houses were summer homes, and were left empty during the winter months.

At my own house I had installed cameras to make sure my aging mother was safe when I was on the road. Dorothea liked the idea, so we installed a few cameras to test it out. When I asked her if she wanted Rosemary to have access, she adamantly refused; she wanted me to be her security monitor. At the same time, I installed a couple of Alexa units so that she could check the weather, find out the time, ask Alexa questions, and play games. Alexa could also be used to call 911 if she had an emergency. We installed the security system during my stay over Christmas 2018.

Once again, in 2019, Dorothea's family accused me of further alienating her from them by installing the cameras. They included the camera installation in their list of charges against me, never acknowledging that it was Dorothea who had prevented them from accessing and monitoring the security system. Behind Dorothea's back, Rosemary asked me for access to the security cameras. But Dorothea had explicitly told me not to give her access. Dorothea never asked me to give, or told me to give Rosemary or anyone else access to the cameras. Therefore, I respected her wishes. Rosemary was not my friend, Dorothea was, and it was Dorothea's home and property. I was not in any kind of position to go against the homeowner. And Rosemary was not entitled to have access to the security system that was bought and paid for by Dorothea, which would be called an invasion of privacy. Rosemary did not have legal authority to override Dorothea. Rosemary was upset that she was denied access and control of Dorothea's security cameras.

Now living in separate states, Dorothea and I communicated mainly by emails, phone calls, texts, and the alerts of her security system in case something went wrong. I still drove more than 700 miles every month to visit her for a few days.

At Sunset Beach, with the help of neighbors who referred a cleaning lady who offered a bi-weekly cleaning program, and a gardener for maintenance of the surroundings, Dorothea arranged for these individuals to assist her. I cooked and labeled food with dates so that she would know what was in the refrigerator. I put her in touch with a group of retired women in the area who met monthly at a local cafe for lunch. One of the most important things I advised her to do was to find a primary care physician as soon as possible so that her medical needs, particularly her B12 deficiency, would be monitored and addressed. Knowing that she still mourned Mary Anne's loss, I suggested she join a grief-counseling group at a local church, but she never did.

The first couple of months of Dorothea's life as a full retiree in her Sunset Beach home were promising. She went out to eat with friends and neighbors, enrolled in a local website to keep in contact with her neighbors, and seemed to take care of herself.

In early spring 2019 however, signs of a downward spiral began to appear. From phone calls, emails, and occasional checks of the security system, I observed things that were a little worrisome.

I noticed what appeared to be a pattern forming regarding her previous B12 deficiency; she became forgetful again. She wrote wrong numbers on a couple of checks; she forgot to replace the batteries in her TV remote and couldn't watch TV for a few days; she switched the table lamps off manually, which threw off the timers, and then she didn't know how to reset the timers. She asked me where to find a few little things in the house. Her eating habits deteriorated to eating crackers because the microwave setup was different from the one, to which she was accustomed. Some days beginning at 1:30 P.M., she would drink six or seven glasses of wine. She did not shower for days, wore the same clothes every day, and stopped taking her walks outside. The cameras caught her sleeping at 4:30 in the afternoon and waking up in the middle of the night. On two occasions she tripped and fell, and on April 15 she fell and the security cameras alerted me to her moving about on the floor. I immediately called a neighbor who ran over to assist.

All these things were signals that she was feeling lonely and not taking good care of herself, and this worried me. Her loneliness was also expressed in her recurring phone calls asking me to visit her at Sunset Beach, although I had continued my monthly trips to visit her. In addition, she repeatedly invited me to move to North Carolina. Once more, I had to make clear that living with her was out of the question because my elderly mother was my primary responsibility.

I was in daily contact with Dorothea, and I was the only person who was aware of Dorothea's B12 pattern of behavior. My emails prove how I reminded her that she could improve her lonely life by eating properly, socializing, controlling her drinking habits, and making sure she managed her B12 deficiency. Rosemary and her family were not aware of Dorothea's behavioral changes because they had practically no contact with her. The last time they had seen Dorothea in person was in Florida, in July 2018.

People who have worked with the elderly are keenly aware of seniors' approach to daily living. In general, seniors don't sweat since they don't exert a lot of energy doing vigorous activity. Therefore, they don't feel the need to shower every day, or they wait to put their clothes in the laundry basket until after they have worn them a couple of times. They get tired of having to cook every day and don't like eating alone, so they just snack. Sometimes they nap in the afternoon, which can mess up their nighttime sleep patterns. Seniors are prone to taking many medications that sometimes have unexpected side effects. Although these traits are common among seniors, some people have a stake in interpreting these symptomatic behaviors as "dementia" so that they can gain access to guardianship. Many of us experienced these same behaviors during the pandemic, yet no one claimed we had sudden onset dementia. We just weren't meeting and socializing with others on a daily basis, and our basic routines and expectations deteriorated.

In today's world, Rosemary could have easily swooped down and claimed Dorothea had Alzheimer's at that time, she would have had much twisted ammunition to interpret Dorothea's behavior as dementia, to accelerate the process for placing her under complete guardianship. I often warned Dorothea that not taking care of herself could be interpreted as such and could be used against her.

Looking back in 2017, when Rosemary drove Dorothea to Sunset Beach, she had attempted to leave Dorothea in North Carolina permanently. Dorothea's return for Mary Anne's interment, and yearlong apartment stay had postponed Rosemary's expectations. This so enraged Rosemary that she began premeditated and malicious allegations against me. In May 2019 it became obvious that Rosemary and her family had

decided that Dorothea belonged in an assisted living facility in Florida. In hindsight, it was the beginning of a months-long scheme to gain control of Dorothea by obtaining guardianship.

Rosemary showed her intentions when she emailed Dorothea links to the websites of three assisted living facilities in Florida. Dorothea answered with, "Nice Rosemary. Thanks!" Rosemary asked her if she liked any of them, and she answered, "Did like them indeed. Thanks again!" Then Rosemary asked her if she had clicked on the pictures that showed floor plans and if she understood that the facilities allowed pets. Dorothea did not respond. Was her refusal to answer a signal to Rosemary that she was not interested?

Throughout the two years of my contact with Dorothea, I had never heard her express a desire to retire in Florida or to any retirement facility for that matter. It was always her plan to move to North Carolina. She told me she had friends there, she knew her neighbors, and, as she put it, "there are things I can be involved in." She had her mind set on retiring to the Sunset Beach summer home.

She was now six months in her dream house. In the beginning she adjusted well, but in the spring, things started to go awry. She was aware that her family wanted her to move to a facility in Florida. The wolves were at the door; in fact, they were at the front door.

June 2019: The Beginning of the End

The month of June 2019 was going to be the worst month in my life. The years of helping Dorothea in building a life of happy retirement were about to come to a crashing end.

It is important to explain the June episode in great detail because it shows how Dorothea's family, the Sunset Beach Police Department, lawyers, and others collaborated to make sure Dorothea ended up in an assisted living facility in Florida, and I ended up in jail.

Fearing a return of the B12 deficiency, I made the trip to North Carolina over the Memorial Day weekend, picked up Dorothea and headed directly to the ER. Once there, they performed a full medical work up. Dorothea had failed to get a primary care physician, despite my insisting that she talk to neighbors and get a reference for a good doctor. The ER diagnosis was conclusive, the B12 deficiency had returned, and she would now be required to get B12 shots for the rest of her life. She was otherwise completely healthy.

On June 6, Dorothea was taken to a local clinic to meet her new doctor by her most trusted neighbor, Gary. He lived five doors from Dorothea, had keys to her house, and was a member of the neighborhood watch group. In an email from June 2019, he related what happened on that day.

The doctor stated that there were no problems besides Dorothea's B12 deficiency. He gave her a B12 shot and told her to come back in a week.

Rosemary had promised to visit Sunset Beach with her two daughters, Courtney and Megan, in early June 2019. As was her habit, she canceled again. She finally arrived with Megan on June 10 and stayed until

June 14. Dorothea must have been excited about their impending arrival, as she had $3,000 transferred from her savings to her checking account, intending to give them each $1,000.

Dorothea's phone calls to me during the visit indicated that it was not going well. Dorothea had anticipated spending time sightseeing with them, but they had other plans, and would not leave the home. The security system footage would later confirm this.

On June 12, Gary went to Dorothea's house to remind her of the June 13 doctor's appointment. Rosemary stated that she could not take Dorothea to the doctor. Dorothea said that she preferred Gary to accompany her anyway.

Early on June 13, Gary arrived to take Dorothea to the doctor. For some reason, Rosemary changed her mind and accompanied them. During the visit Rosemary had the opportunity to speak to the doctor about Dorothea's B12 issues, but Dorothea told me that she chose not to do so; she stayed with Gary in the waiting room.

Upon returning home, during the conversation between Rosemary and Gary, Rosemary said, "We are moving anyway." When Gary asked Rosemary if her family was moving, she said, "No, we are taking Dorothea to Florida," to which Dorothea retorted, "We will see about that!" She had told Gary on several occasions that she did not want to move to Florida. Less than 24 hours later, Rosemary and Megan returned to Florida.

Dorothea's distressing calls stating that, "things did not go well" had made me decide to visit her. When I arrived in Sunset Beach after midnight on Saturday, June 15, I found the house in disarray. The condition of the house was out of the ordinary for Dorothea, as she was very much a creature of habit, liking things tight and neat, with everything in its place. Her environment had been rearranged, even a painting on the wall had been removed and Rosemary had replaced it with photos of her

64

children. It's important to note that Dorothea only had photos of her mother and father displayed on her nightstand in the Glen Arm home, the apartment and then in the Sunset Beach home. Rosemary added photos even on the nightstand.

I reviewed the security system videos, which revealed that within an hour after their arrival, Rosemary and her daughter were telling Dorothea that she should move to Florida. "Florida! Florida! Come live in Florida!" they shouted. The audio revealed that they berated her, her choices, and me. "So, seriously, you keep balking, do you really not want to move to Florida? You are living with someone that you take out for every meal." At one point Megan said to her, "You look sad . . . but Mom is doing this for you."

The cameras showed that, while Dorothea was at the doctor's office, Megan was making phone calls to nursing facilities in Florida, inquiring about availability and giving personal information about her aunt. There was also security footage showing Megan taking photos of Dorothea's logins, passwords, credit cards, and other papers.

On the third day of their visit, security footage showed Dorothea drinking wine early in the day. On the stamped security video Rosemary can be heard saying, "Another thing: I think we should go to the bank, and uh, we should get me on your account." A few minutes later she said, "The place closes in like twenty minutes." Dorothea agreed to go. When Dorothea went to get her purse, security footage showed Rosemary doing a little "happy dance." The morning after the bank visit, Rosemary and her daughter left for Florida.

What I had gathered from the security system made me very concerned about Dorothea's well-being: the insistence of her sister on bringing Dorothea to Florida, the contacts with assisted living facilities, the berating, the copying of personal information, and the rush to go to the bank and place Rosemary on her bank accounts. If Rosemary had a valid POA drawn up in June 2017, she would already have had access to

Dorothea's accounts in case Dorothea was incapacitated. She would not need to insist on the bank visit. And what was that "happy dance" about?

My concern was so great that I tried to contact the Sunset Beach Police Department but was unsuccessful. Then I tried via Facebook, as I had done in the past, but they did not respond.

Later that morning, on June 15, it became clear that the visit had upset Dorothea. As generous as Dorothea was, I noticed that she never gave them the money she had set aside for their visit.

In an attempt to calm Dorothea down, and return to some normalcy, we decided to relax and went sightseeing, did some putting, walked on the beach, and I cooked dinner on the grill.

At some point that evening, Rosemary's oldest daughter Courtney called Dorothea to tell her that her nephew Michael was flying in because he was worried about her. This was followed by a seemingly unending series of calls and answering machine messages from family members and others who "wanted to make sure she was all right." On Saturday I called 911 around 9:10 P.M., informing them that it was not an immediate emergency but that there might be a domestic disturbance that might require assistance.

We later learned from Michael himself that he had had no plans to fly to Sunset Beach; he was at a wedding that weekend. To put this into perspective, Rosemary routinely would call the next-door neighbor on Friday or Saturday and inquire if I was visiting Dorothea. Periodically, the neighbor would tell us of these phone inquiries. Apparently, this was the result of one of the inquiries, a slew of harassing phone calls that actually frighten Dorothea. If anyone was to check the phone records, they would see that these family members only called Dorothea after a special occasion to thank her for a check she had sent them. Her brother who had not spoken to her since July 2018 even left a message on her voice mail. Rosemary's son, Logan, suddenly wanted to call her on a regular basis because he said he enjoyed their conversation the previous day. One niece who sounded like she was trying to speak to a three-year old, told her how she had just graduated from college and named her degree. These calls had long pauses in them as if they were talking to someone else next to them, before they finished a sentence. They were all very odd. One right after another. And even though relatives had spoken to Dorothea, they continued to call as if they hadn't. At one point Dorothea looked at me and said, "Why are they doing this? They never call me." "I don't know, but I think they want to try to record you saying something that they may use against you later."

While at dinner on Sunday, Dorothea noticed that her wallet was in total disarray: cards in the wrong slots, cards upside down. Returning to Dorothea's house, I found her checkbook in a computer bag in the kitchen, a very unusual place indeed, and noticed that one of the blank checks was missing and was not logged on the back of the checkbook, as was Dorothea's habit.

At some point, after reviewing the camera footage, I showed Dorothea the security footage described above. Concluding that private documents, including passwords and ID's that had been found in their safe place, had been tampered with and photographed during the visit, we decided to go to the sheriff's department the following day.

Dorothea told me that the repeated phone calls frightened her. She was afraid to leave her home for fear of what she would find upon her return. Usually, the family called her only on special occasions and holidays.

At 9:00 A.M., on Monday, deputy sheriff Ryan Sheppard spoke with Dorothea in person. She told him that she feared being forcibly removed from her home by Rosemary and Michael. The sheriff took a four-page report and gave her handwritten directions to the courthouse to have a protective order placed on Rosemary.[4] I promised to get him a copy of the security camera footage, but explained I just had no knowledge of how to do that at the time, since this was the first time, we were required to do this.

Before going to the courthouse, Dorothea stopped at the bank. She told the bank manager about her concerns that her wallet had been rifled through, cards were mixed up, and she was missing a check.

For some reason, maybe because she had been drinking, or maybe it was the increased stress Rosemary placed upon her, she did not remember being at the bank the previous Thursday and putting Rosemary on her account as POA. *Was her B12 deficiency acting up?* She asked the bank manager what a POA was, and after he explained it she stated that she did not want her sister to have any access to her finances.

She created three new accounts and had her funds transferred from the old accounts, where Rosemary was a joint account holder, into the new accounts, which were in Dorothea's name only. She canceled her old credit and debit cards and got new ones. The bank manager reminded her that she would have to redirect her monthly Social Security checks and see to it that her automated deposits could access the new accounts. She also requested that her new checks be mailed to her next-door neighbor because she might be in Baltimore, Maryland, when they arrived.

We then proceeded to the courthouse, where we learned that all the judges were at a convention on June 17. They told us to return the next day.

We get in the truck, and something tells me that we need to call the investment advisor, and tell him what's going on. I give Dorothea the phone and she makes the call to alert him that her passwords and ID were

---

[4] This report was closed as being "unfounded" when I was placed in jail. Out of jail, I attempted twice to contact the Deputy Sheriff Ryan Shepard who had talked to Dorothea, but he never returned my calls.

compromised, while Rosemary had visited the previous week. He tells Dorothea that Rosemary has already been in contact with him and has changed the passwords on Dorothea's account, earlier that morning based on a request from Rosemary. But due to the accusations he is hearing, he is requesting from his top-level investment security that all activity is stopped and all access will be locked down. We are in total agreement that the account needs to be locked down. We thank him for securing Dorothea's investments.

As we're leaving the parking lot, on our way back home, we called Dorothea's original lawyer in Towson, who had created the POA for Rosemary in June 2017. Here is that conversation, which I wrote down, and have repeated to many people as it is the oddest phone call I have ever been on.

"Hi, my name is Pam. I'm with Dorothea. I'd like to speak to Dorothea's lawyer. We are trying to find out when the most recent POA was created and signed by Dorothea."

A male voice responded: "It was 06/05/2017. But I can't speak to you. I need to speak to Dorothea."

Dorothea whispers softly that she thinks her lawyer went to Notre Dame Prep. This made me pause, because the person who was speaking was a male. Dorothea took the phone and said, "Hello."

The male voice said, "Well, I really have no way of determining if you are who you say you are."

We put the phone on speaker, and I said, "I can photo her driver's license and take a photo of her and send it."

The male voice yelled back to Dorothea, "Will you tell her to shut up. I can't hear you with her yelling in the background," he said rudely. He then asked, "Where are you?"

69

Dorothea answered, "In a truck traveling to Maryland.

"Great, you can make an appointment and see me when you get in town."

Dorothea asked, "Where are you?"

He replied, "In Towson. How about tomorrow for an appointment?"

I felt that something was wrong and signaled to Dorothea to stop the call. I pulled off to the roadside and googled Dorothea's lawyer, and learned that she was a female, not the male who impersonated her on the phone. It later turned out that the 06/05/2017 POA had never been certified by the courts and it was Dorothea's lawyer's boss, the person who had talked to us, who was a partner in the law firm, and who had answered the other lawyer's personal cell phone.

It just got more and more convoluted as Rosemary reeled in more and more people to believe her lies. My head is spinning at this point. I'm texting all kinds of friends hoping they can offer us some kind of insight or advice.

Dorothea says to me, "A couple of things before we leave for Maryland, Pam. I want you to change the locks on the house and tell Gary not to give the keys to anyone in my family." That quickly, we headed off to the hardware store for new locks for the house. It is a total whirlwind of accusation after accusation being hurled at us, while Dorothea continues to try to tell people that Rosemary is making all the stories up.

That night, after the locks were changed, we worked together on drafting a letter to be left behind at the summer home, because Dorothea feared Rosemary would attempt to sell her home. Dorothea wanted anyone working with Rosemary to know there would be consequences, believing Rosemary's lies and working alongside her, and against

Dorothea. Strange enough, the letter in which all of Dorotheas fears expressed in the letter, have come true, was also submitted by the police to the Assistant District Attorney, somehow as evidence against me. The document is as follows:

To Whom It May Concern,

This is to inform all who are involved with Rosemary, my half-sister, who is 20 years younger than I, and who has recently announced herself as my active POA, without my knowledge. She has lost my trust as my POA, since she has jumped the gun on assuming her duties as my POA and has refused to follow my wishes as required from my POA. She has refused to listen to my neighbors, my doctors and my friends, who all agree that although I am 77 years old, with minor health issues, I am not unable or impaired anywhere near the degree where a POA is required for decision making.

Avoid doing business with Rosemary. My property is not at her disposal. And she will be held personally and financially accountable for any property and personal documents that are sold or given away and/ or removed from [my Sunset Beach property]. She will also be held personally accountable for any financial expenditures she makes from my accounts.

The Sunset Beach Sherifs Department, the Brunswick County Police Department, the Brunswick county court clerk and the Department of Social Services Elder Abuse are all aware and involved.

This is under litigation. You have been warned.

I have no plans to move to Florida. I do not want to move to Florida. It was never even a passing thought to move to Florida. I am happy where I am. I love my house, my neighbors, and my community. My mortgage is paid off. I am financially secure and fully expect to live out my retirement in Sunset Beach North Carolina. Anything else is not following my directives and wishes. I will not be forced out of my home on the whim of control from my half-sister.

Sincerely,

Dorothea

The next day, Wednesday, June 18, we returned to the courthouse around 10:00 A.M. only to be told to come back around 1:00 P.M. The courthouse is about an hour from her home, so we inquired about senior resources and were directed to another building. We went there, Dorothea met a social worker, who took a report, but concluded that since I was accompanying Dorothea, even though I was merely visiting from out of state, I still qualified as her advocate, so they were unable to assist her. *It is important to note, all documents were subpoenaed from Social Services, but this report went missing, and they denied having any such document. However, the December 2021 subpoena is how I learned that Rosemary had filed a report with social services on June 20, 2019, repeating her false allegations to them against me.* We left Social Services and entered the cafeteria, grabbed a plate of food and sat down to eat. I immediately found the food to be horrible and threw it out. Dorothea, on the other hand, cleaned her plate. We continued on our way to the court clerk's office, but just prior to getting there Dorothea got sick and spewed everywhere in the lady's room. I needed to take her back home, she wasn't feeling well and her clothes were a mess. The Clerk was busy so I wrote a note that Dorothea had become ill, adding that a janitor was needed in the lady's restroom, and that Dorothea would return the following day. However, when the judge became available that day, and Dorothea wasn't nearby, a judge ordered a court date hearing to be set to file the protective order against Rosemary, rather than wait for Dorothea to return the next day and issue a temporary restraining order. The lack of the protective order ended up being a huge detriment to Dorothea.

At 8:00 A.M. on June 19th, Gary arrived to pick up Dorothea for her weekly B12 shot at the doctor's office. I met Dorothea and Gary afterwards at the clinic parking lot.

"I made a record of the visit, Pam. She got her B12 shot," Gary said, "and the doctor stated that her memory issues were the result from her B12 deficiency. She might need some assistance but does not require 24/7 care. Dorothea is able to make her own decisions."

"Good news, Gary, that's exactly what I have always maintained. Anything else?"

"Yes, he said that she should not be alone as much and should make an appointment with a neurologist, but it was not urgent. He also mentioned that he had reservations about the specifics of the cognitive tests and thought they were antiquated." After the visit, Dorothea seemed happier.

"Are we ready to go to Maryland?" she asked. "I am looking forward to seeing my friends there again."

"You'll see your friends, Dorothea, and an attorney. But first we have to return once more to the courthouse, to pick up your paperwork." Unfortunately, we learned that Dorothea's only option was to accept the judge's set hearing date, for the middle of the following week.

This is Dorothea's statement on the Complaint and Motion for Domestic Violence Protective Order:

"My sister came to visit and while she was here, she started to harass and verbally assaulting [sic] me. She was in my face pointing her finger in my face. She stole from me and forced me to give her financial control of my finances. She left to go back home but told me she was going to be back and make me to go to Florida with her. I am afraid of her and what she will do if and when she comes back. I am afraid she could physically assault me and force me to get in a car with her. I don't want her to come back to my home. I want her to have no contact with me."

End of statement.

When an individual needs protection, it shouldn't come with a 7+ day wait. This was an epic court system failure, further allowing Rosemary to continue her false allegations, which would soon end up crossing state lines.

About five hours into our trip, a neighbor called to inform us that Dorothea's brother Ricky, and his two adult sons David and Michael, were at Dorothea's home in North Carolina with the Sunset Beach police.

I immediately got in touch with the Sunset Beach Police Department through Facebook and told the detective in charge, Detective Jared Cox, that Dorothea had filed a report with the sheriff, that there was a court date for a protective order against Rosemary, and that Dorothea had spoken to the Department of Social Services. I told him that I was law enforcement, and that Dorothea was safe. He asked what agency I was with, and I replied Maryland State Police/ Office of the State Fire Marshal. I told him my boss would call him and confirm my identity and job. Cox told me, "Awesome!"

As we later would learn, that "awesome" took a U-turn when, at the behest of Rosemary and based on a list of charges against me, Detective Cox requested a fugitive and felony warrant for my arrest, and while speaking to Baltimore County police, he told them that I blew him off stating, "Go pound sand" (a phrase I had never heard before). Sunset Beach Police Department would later say that they had asked me to return to North Carolina, but they never made that request. It's a good thing the entire conversation with Cox is in text format. Had it been a phone call, he could have made up anything in the same manner as Rosemary, and gotten away with it. However, everything I have, has been saved electronically and on paper.

And so, at the intentionally misleading request for a felony warrant, I became a fugitive and a felon, where Baltimore County Police Department sting-rayed my cell phone. This meant they triangulated my cell phone to figure out where I was located in Maryland. Thereafter, there were attempts to hack my email accounts; those hack attempts continued for several months. I have screenshots and Google supplied IP addresses.

Detective Cox further contacted the sheriff's department in Sunset Beach and had a deputy close Dorothea's initial gaslighting report, calling it "unfounded." Detective Cox failed to get bank statements from the bank proving no money was missing. Finally, he told the Assistant District Attorney that I had impersonated a police officer.

On Thursday, June 20, the day after we arrived at my mother's Baltimore home where I lived, I needed to do some fire inspections. Dorothea was my guest, and I would not leave her under the care of my elderly mother. Dorothea was curious to see what my job entailed, so I invited her to accompany me on a few safety inspections.

After she went to her stylist for a haircut, we attempted to contact her former neighbor-lawyer, but we were unsuccessful. We did, however, leave business cards, with a note at her address. We visited Notre Dame Prep to interact with familiar faces who could be witnesses attesting to Dorothea's health and well-being. Dorothea spoke to one of the nuns about her fear that her half-sister was attempting to force her to move to Florida. She also explained that she and I had come to Maryland to obtain legal advice.

Back at my mother's home, we completed the written statements we had begun in North Carolina, including her letter spelling out her retirement plans, but being so late in the day, we could not find a notary to notarize them. Fearing the proverbial "next shoe to drop", Dorothea read a written statement in front of two neighbors and told everyone those were her wishes, and the two neighbors also read and signed her typed statement, as witnesses.

That written statement is as follows:

"This document is to confirm my retirement intentions, and any subsequent health care initiatives. This is to be used as a guide to any person I have currently or will designate in the future as my POA. My plans have always been to retire in my home in Sunset Beach, NC. Mary Anne and I purchased the property and built the house with that retirement intention. My plans have not changed. When I am no longer able to care for myself, or when my mobility or health may be compromised temporarily (as stipulated by my attending physician), I want health care aide in my home. I do not want to be moved to a nursing, or assisted living facility. My wish is to live and in the end, die in my current home. I am financially secure enough to make this my intention, and for health care to be provided to me within my home. Sincerely, Dorothea."

In the early evening, there was a knock on the door. Opening it, I faced two police officers and suddenly more officers appeared from behind trees and across the street, some with rifles and others holding riot shields.

Surprised, I said, "Really? All you had to do is ask. I want to talk to you guys."

They announced that they had a warrant for my arrest for extortion. They slapped handcuffs on my wrists and sat me on a chair on the porch. One of my neighbors who had witnessed the whole scene, quipped, "There were three old ladies in the house, and they show up with a SWAT team?"

For a while the police officers seemed confused. One officer told me, "You are arrested because you did not make a phone call."

"Huh? A phone call?" Another officer walked towards me from the street and added, "Do you know why you are being arrested?" With a confused and squished up face I replied, "Not really." Now I was looking back at the first officer who had blamed it on lack of a phone call. The second officer then told me that the reason for my arrest was extortion.

"Extortion! Wow, that's a new one. How in the world?" I yelled to my neighbor.

He yelled back, "Isn't that what her sister is doing to her?"

The word "extortion," the display of a SWAT team, and my handcuffs had stunned me. I couldn't help thinking how ridiculous the whole situation was.

Now even the police seemed confused. One officer asked, "Who is the auxiliary police officer?" I replied, "I am. Or was, until I retired in January." Another officer was shaking his head saying, "There is something wrong with this, but we cannot unarrest you after you are arrested."

An officer walked me to the cruiser, and without thinking I went to sit in the front seat just out of habit, the officer and I both chuckled. I glanced back at the house. Dorothea and my mother were both standing helpless outside on the front porch, trying to comprehend the whole fiasco. They both looked dumbfounded. Before the police cruiser took off, I pleaded with several different officers to protect Dorothea. They said they would, but they failed to do so. My pleas for help fell on deaf ears.

As auxiliary police, my neighbors had seen me come and go from my house, for years in an official police uniform. Now, the sleepy little cul-de-sac with a heavy police presence of multiple cars lining the street, and officers with rifles and riot shields, crossing neighbors' yards had made many of my neighbors come out of their homes, curious to learn what was going on.

Sitting in the back of the police car in handcuffs, viewing my neighbors holding cell phones recording the event, was humiliating. This is what happens to criminals, not innocent people helping their friends. How could this happen? How could Rosemary with the help of police, now put two elderly women at risk? I was so naive to think I'd be back home in 24 hours, even if I had to walk the few blocks to protect my mom and my friend. Little did I know it would be nine days and I would be stuck in North Carolina, 700 miles away. It would be days before I would even go before a judge and be denied bail. Then I had to wait for the Sunset Beach Police to arrive to extradite me back to North Carolina. I just wanted to get this overwith, and tell the authorities what was truly going on, and get protection for Dorothea from her half-sister.

Over a four-day period following my arrest, and while I was still in jail, in the County, Michael, David and Ricky traveled Maryland and repeatedly made daily calls to police requesting wellness checks on Dorothea. These were more harassing than the phone calls they placed to Dorothea beginning on June 15th through June 17th, because with each call, the police would arrive at my mother's home and demand to speak to everyone. Each time my mother and Dorothea told the police they were fine and there was no cause to continue the harassment. Each day, the three men also arrived to physically intimidate the women. During these wellness checks, the police allowed Michael to, not only come onto the property, but he was allowed to remain on the front porch and participate in harassing the two elderly women as well. The women refused to open the storm door, fearing the police would enter the home and remove them as well. Unknown to the police, was the fact that the storm door had a broken handle lock, and the door was merely secured by an eye hook.

On body cam footage two officers can be heard discussing how they should attempt to bring the women out of the house to gain custody of Dorothea. It was very disheartening, to later learn through viewing police body cam video, that the police were acting on false statements from Michael saying he had POA, and he waved a document around, as if it was court certified when it wasn't. He was intentionally misleading the police, to gain control of Dorothea. The untrained police accepted the document without recognizing it required a court seal to be accepted as a legal document, to the detriment of Dorothea.

The officers then instructed Michael that the one way he could extract Dorothea was to seek legal advice to get an emergency medical evaluation approved by the court. On June 24, authorities failed to protect Dorothea, after Michael lied in Baltimore County court, saying Dorothea was failing to take her medication, and because of that, she was an immediate danger to herself and others.

This is a known "line" many senior daycare centers "feed" to 911 to get medics to take that days "problem client" to the hospital, because they don't want to deal with the client having a bad day.

When police arrived to remove Dorothea from my mother's house, Dorothea asked, "Will you bring me back here?" The officer said, "Yes." Dorothea left the home begrudgingly, with just her purse and the clothes on her back. The judge ultimately handed Dorothea over to Michael, David and Ricky in Towson, after she was released from an emergency medical evaluation. The officer left soon after he deposited Dorothea at the hospital, and after instructing Michael what to do. Again, this was detrimental to Dorothea. The police did not protect her from the very people she reported that she feared. They did not attempt to learn whose side the evaluation benefitted. We have no idea what the medical staff was told by Michael. We can assume that he told them, exactly what he told police, as seen on police body cam footage, that Dorothea was kidnapped, and that a woman whom she had trusted had stolen $125K from her and had been arrested, and that Dorothea was in denial.

So, three days later, when the court hearing for the protective order in North Carolina scheduled for June 27th rolled around, no one showed up, and Dorothea's motion was automatically denied. They essentially kidnapped her, and refuse to allow her to go to a court ordered hearing, for a restraining order against them. Should the Baltimore Police have known about the court hearing for a protective order? They did.

They were told about the court date several times by my mother and Dorothea. A county police officer actually instructed Michael how to get around it, after he dropped Dorothea off at the hospital. Again, county police failed to protect the elderly woman. Their actions were to the detriment of Dorothea. Everyone acted on emotion, not facts.

While I remained jailed in Baltimore, the North Carolina Department of Social Services did a follow-up wellness check, to Dorothea's home, based on Rosemary's phone call to them on June 20th, this was not based on the in-person interview Dorothea made to them in their office at the Brunswick County Government Building on June 17th. They spoke to Rosemary, who was in the process of filing the paperwork for guardianship over Dorothea. Rosemary told them that I had been arrested and was in jail and that she would take Dorothea to Florida with her. The DSS agent told an inquisitive neighbor that she couldn't remove Dorothea from her home and that she needed to get a lawyer.[5] My question was, if they knew Dorothea feared the family, why couldn't they get the police to remove the family from Dorothea's home? It was, after all, Dorothea's home, not Rosemary's. Rosemary still didn't have a POA with a court seal certifying the document she and Michael presented to authorities. My other question was, how were they allowed to get a lock smith to gain entrance into the home prior to Dorothea arriving in N.C? The security cameras captured the break-in.

Rosemary's Protective Service report repeats some of the charges she had filed with the police. Here are a few: she falsely claims that I took Dorothea off Aricept for dementia; that I visited Dorothea weekly in North Carolina; that I transferred $125,000 to another account and it was missing; and that I was taking advantage of Dorothea's money and was guilty of exploitation.

---

[5] The DSS never attempted to remove Michael or Rosemary from Dorothea's home, even though she reported being fearful of them and their intentions.

The report also paints a very negative picture of Dorothea: she cannot remember how to use the microwave; she has no transportation; she has memory loss; she sometimes "says mean things"; she drinks; and she has incontinence, weight, and skin problems. She cannot prepare meals, take medication, take care of her money, or do housekeeping, and she has problems making phone calls.

Rosemary's Protective Service report was not accepted for evaluation because the family had come to North Carolina and had gone to the police department to "act on Dorothea's behalf." Rosemary had a POA and would have the ability to contact the banks.

Felon and Fugitive

The police drove me to the precinct to book me. I spent the night wearing shorts, a polo shirt, and flip flops. My ankles were placed in shackles. The small jail cell was painted, cinderblock, and cinderblock was also the bench on which to sit or sleep. All night I was hoping that Dorothea was safe in my mother's house, and I thought about the families I had scheduled for fire inspections.

The events of my arrest kept repeating in my head. I realized that the police had never read me, my Miranda rights. Although an arresting police officer does not have to read the Miranda rights when they have a warrant, they must read the arrestee's rights during an interrogation. But they never interrogated me. This meant that they could not take anything I might have said after my arrest and use it against me. Not that I had said anything incriminating, but so far, everything others had said against me were false. And no one was listening to me or Dorothea.

My feelings were raw. I felt like someone had punched me in the gut, and I had the wind knocked out, and had a lump in my throat, as if I was about to throw up. I had a pounding headache and racing thoughts of sadness. This feeling would plague me for a long time, at least a year and a half. I had an overwhelming sense of anger at the Sunset Beach police, Rosemary, Michael, and "the System."

Where would I go from here? Could I still trust anyone? The surveillance of my cell phone and attempts to hack my emails had made me paranoid. To whom could I turn for help? Would it matter to anyone besides my mother that I was sitting in jail? People relied on me; I didn't rely on others for help. How would those who I had always helped, be able to not only get along without me, but how could they ever help me? I was alone. My thoughts were bouncing all over the place, hopelessness in all directions.

Having never been on the other side of the law except for a few speeding tickets, I was now considered a fugitive with a felony charge. The following morning, they continued the booking that the night shift had failed to complete for some reason. I was allowed to make a phone call to my mother. I asked her to get in touch with Dorothea's neighbor, the lawyer, and request legal help.

Two plain-clothes officers placed me in an unmarked cruiser to bring me from the precinct to the Towson Detention Center. They admitted they had never told any detainee this before, but said that they truly hoped everything would work out for me and that they just didn't believe the accusations against me. Amid the avalanche of uncertainty and humiliation since my arrest, their compassion touched me deeply.

At the detention center, I entered a huge room, joining about a hundred people in handcuffs and shackles. From there I was placed with two other people in a smaller room with cement block ledges on which to sit. My name was called to meet the medical technicians. I had to go through the humiliation of being strip-searched and wearing handcuffs and leg shackles.

I had to answer questions about my medical history, and when I told them I had never been incarcerated, they looked at me as if I was lying. Then they gave me the obligatory tetanus shot.

The Sunset Beach Police had requested my extradition to North Carolina. I readily signed the extradition papers to make sure I could face my accusers in that state. At this point, having read the actual charges, I cried. I told those around me that I was not the one who was deceiving Dorothea; her own family was.

Throughout my incarceration, I was allowed to make timed phone calls to my mother.

I learned in 2020 when the North Carolina Assistant District Attorney handed over Discovery, that the phone calls were recorded, but somehow only an interpretation of segments of some of the conversations were given to me in text format. No one explained to

me, how the text format came to be. Had the Baltimore County Police communicated the content of these conversations to the Sunset Beach Police, or had the Sunset Beach Police just cherry-picked sentences they thought were juicy? How did they become part of the charging documents? How these phone calls were reported and interpreted remained unclear. But the Sunset Beach Police gave just a few sentences (taken out of context) to the Assistant District Attorney to make it appear as if it was incriminating evidence. It wasn't. In those phone calls were conversations to my 91-year-old mom, about where my mom could locate evidence to prove my innocence, and my fear concerning Dorothea's safety. If the Sunset Beach Police had followed up on the contents of the phone calls, and investigated the leads they would have learned of the truth early on. Quite the opposite actually occurred. The Sunset Beach Police, upon hearing the phone conversations, failed to secure evidence. Was this intentional? Why?

If the family had managed to get me arrested, what would prevent them from taking Dorothea to Florida and gaining guardianship over her?

They placed me in a cell unit for first timers and non-violent drug users. Each individual cell was just big enough for one steel bunk bed, a steel stool, a small table anchored into the wall, and a steel toilet attached to a sink. If the constant anxiety wasn't enough, the one-inch-thick plastic-coated mattress guaranteed more sleepless nights lay ahead.

The cell doors were kept open all day, so there was no privacy. Correctional staff sat in a nearby observation station. The food that was rolled in on trays was mostly unidentifiable and smelled foul. I survived by eating some pieces of bread, cookies, fruit, and drink pouches, but had diarrhea the entire time I was there.

On Sunday, June 23, I met Dorothea's neighbor, the lawyer, through a glass window. She said she would try to get me bail. The next day, I had a court appearance along with many other detainees who lined up and waited to be called in front of the judge in another part of the detention center. One by one, cases were heard before the judge, sheriffs made statements, and the judge issued a ruling. When my turn came, my lawyer attempted to get me bail, but it was denied. The sheriff told the judge that the Sunset Beach Police had initially said that they would pick me up 24 hours after I waived extradition. But The Sunset Beach Police now asked the judge for a longer hold, until after July 5. The judge found their request unreasonable and required Sunset Beach Police to pick me up before June 30 or he would release me. A couple men who were awaiting a hearing with the same judge I had just seen, were laughing at the white girl in distress as I returned to my place in line, some women near by told them to shut up, it wasn't funny. Worried about my elderly mother with cataracts who was not set up with groceries, and who couldn't drive to the store, and who had never used a taxi or bus in the last 70 years, was now tasked to protect Dorothea, I cried at a worker's desk in the detention center. She gave me a Kleenex. I was not prepared for this. This was not familiar; this was not where an innocent person belongs. I was treated as a criminal, someone who had harmed another. I had never felt so alone, or vulnerable to harm and danger as I did in there. It was a frightening experience, I had nothing in common with anyone in there. I donned my best mean, "don't mess with me" scowl, and hoped it worked.

Five days after I was incarcerated, my contract with the State Police/State Fire Marshal was terminated. I was served with termination papers while in jail. I learned that the second in command, Greg Der had called the Sunset Beach Police Department and had spoken to assistant chief, Joe Smith. An email from Greg Der to the State Fire Marshal, to my immediate boss, and to the director of personnel, listed the charges against me from the Sunset Beach Police. The email outlined the lies Rosemary had told the police, and the email indicated that the Sunset Beach police told my boss they had investigated the accusations to be true. Nowhere in the list does the word "allegedly" appear in the presentation of "the facts" and the charges—nor is there any proof included or alluded to, of their veracity.

This list of charges and events reflects the allegations made by the family to Detective Cox, to obtain my felony arrest warrant. I will later describe these charges in greater detail, but I want to briefly mention them here in the context of my firing. I am reporting them as they were stated in the email without commenting on them. To get the arrest warrant, Sunset Beach Police misled the North Carolina courts. This was followed by the Sunset Beach Police misleading a county law enforcement agency to get the arrest. The Sunset Beach then went a step further to mislead my state government employer, another law enforcement agency, which got me fired. My unemployment lasted over three years, as a direct result of the false police report filed by Rosemary and the Sunset Beach Police who failed to investigate the accusations.

The following points were part of an email that was placed in my personnel file and ultimately used to terminate my employment:

- *I befriended a local elderly lady, and traveled weekly back and forth between Maryland and North Carolina.*

- *Dorothea is a wealthy lady who suffers from dementia, is a vulnerable adult, with a sister and nephew who live in Texas.*

- *I installed cameras and refused to give the family access.*

- *I went to the bank and attempted to gain access to her accounts. The bank manager suspected something wasn't right and refused to add me to the accounts.*

- *I attempted to get POA through an attorney, who also refused to draft a POA.*

- *At that point, the family contacted authorities.*

- *Through their investigation, Sunset Beach Police gathered evidence that I signed or had Dorothea sign checks for my own benefit.*

- *I identified myself as Maryland State Police.*

- *I drove to South Carolina and brought Dorothea to Maryland.*

The email further states that the Sunset Beach Police's Detective Cox applied for and received a felony warrant for elder abuse, exploitation of the elderly, and several other felonies. Baltimore County police arrested me for the open felony warrant and held me without bond, awaiting extradition back to North Carolina.

These accusations were then repeated in statements by Rosemary and Michael to support their quest for guardianship, to the detriment of Dorothea, who lost all her civil rights as an independent U.S. citizen.

Eight days after I had arrived at the Towson Detention Center on June 29, the Sunset Beach police arrived, put me in handcuffs and leg shackles, and drove me 8 and half hours to Brunswick County Jail, where I was processed through a county criminal intake facility and placed in another jail cell.

It became immediately clear that things were looking up a bit. They told me bail had been set at $10,000, and they gave me a list of bail bondsmen and a phone. I had nothing with me, so I had to rely on my 91-year-old mom to contact the bondsman and make the bail arrangements. Complicating the matter, since I was not a resident of North Carolina, the bondsman required a local co-signer. Dorothea's neighbor Gary, came to the rescue and co-signed the bond with my mother.

While I was waiting in the cell, a hopeless looking woman was placed with me. She took one look at me and said, "Honey, you don't belong in here!" I had to smile, thinking that the two plain clothes county officers had pretty much said the same thing to me as well.

A short time later, a sheriff led me to be interviewed again by medical techs. They had not been given the paperwork I brought with me from Baltimore County, and wanted to give me another tetanus shot. An argument ensued, and my blood pressure must have gone through the roof. I was not going to be injected with a second tetanus shot when I had gotten one just one week prior. They asked if hypertension ran in my family. "No, I don't have high blood pressure," I told them, "but this is my first time in jail." They threatened to put me in restraints if I did not agree to get the injection. This was thoroughly uncalled for, "For Pete's sake, look at the paperwork before making threats about using restraints." In the end, they located the paperwork and backed down, but they weren't even nice about it. The frustration continued. The whole state appeared to have a problem admitting when they were wrong.

At around 1:30 A.M., I was given a towel and maroon scrubs. I was told to strip and apply a strong, very toxic smelling de-licer on my hair and rinse it off in the cold shower. They escorted me to a six-by-ten windowless cell and gave me a one-inch-thick mattress and sheets. All night, as a florescent light burned overhead, the room filled with terrifying sounds: doors sliding and slamming, shoes clomping on stairways, voices yelling, and keys rattling. It was psychologically very disturbing. My guess is that it is intended to be so, at least for the innocent.

In the early morning, breakfast was delivered. I must give credit to the Sheriff's Department for their treatment of detainees, in this respect at least. For the first time in days, I had a real breakfast, with real scrambled eggs, sausage, and pancakes that smelled and tasted as they are supposed to smell and taste.

By 11:30 A.M., I was told to get my mattress and sheets and put them on a pile. They led me to the processing area, where to my surprise, I found the clothing I had been wearing when I was arrested. Upon exiting the room, I saw Gary and the bail bondsman, who had been waiting since 9:30 A.M. I crumpled into Gary's arms in tears.

The agony of ten days and nights in jail cells in two states had crushed my soul. Knowing that I had never exploited Dorothea and was innocent of the charges, had created in me a deep anger at the people who had put me in jail. I knew that it would take a long time to heal from this torment. But at this moment I was exhausted, and I had no idea where to turn, or what my next step was going to be. Navigating through this system had been torture, my mind numb. I was so thankful for Gary's support.

After I signed the paperwork, they told me to stay out of trouble and explained that I had a court appearance scheduled for Monday morning. Gary invited me to stay with him until then. We shopped for some new clothes, rented a car to drive back to Maryland, and made plans to meet a lawyer that Dorothea's former Glen Arm neighbor, the lawyer, had contacted.

At the court hearing I was officially charged with exploitation of an elderly person. As a condition of my bail bond, I could not have any contact with Dorothea or her family and was forbidden from going near her property. I would be required to attend an evidentiary hearing the following month. This would lead to another court date and then another; the Assistant District Attorney would request multiple continuances over the years to come, as is routine for the prosecution in the North Carolina court system.

Being released from jail did not end my troubles. Indeed, it was the beginning of an almost three-year saga of facing ADA Shirley Smircic's abundance of requested continuances of court dates, dealing with lawyers, and gathering as much information as possible to prove my innocence.

The bail bond was hanging over my head. If I sneezed the wrong way, I would end up in a cell again. A speeding ticket or a broken brake light on my truck could land me back behind bars in North Carolina. This is just another horrible harassing thing to hang over an innocent person's head. This lasted for years.

The bail bond also prevented me from renewing my concealed carry permits. As a single, female traveling alone, to and from North Carolina or any other neighboring states, I was unable to protect myself with a legally purchased weapon. How is that "innocent until proven guilty?" The right to "equal the playing field" if attacked, was taken away from me. I was also denied renewal of my passport.

Every week I applied for jobs, many jobs. I received one call back, and when I explained the situation, I was told they could not hire me until the matter was cleared up. All a potential employer had to do was Google my name and state, to read the accusations against me.

The day after my arrest, The Brunswick Beacon newspaper in North Carolina had reported: *"A Baltimore, Maryland, woman has been arrested on a charge of exploitation of a disabled/elderly person's trust in Sunset Beach. On June 20, Sunset Beach police took a report in reference to the cited charges. Later that day warrants were issued for Pam of Baltimore, Maryland (and published my street address as well). When detectives went to the Sunset Beach house, they learned that she had gone to Baltimore, Maryland. She was later arrested at an address in Maryland and awaits extradition back to North Carolina."*

This too, remains a permanent smear on my reputation. In addition, Sunset Beach police filed the charges in the FBI database and refused to remove them, fully knowing all the allegations are false. *Why would they do this to an innocent person? If they are doing it to me, you can bet they have done this in the past to others and gotten away with it.* I will never understand what Detective Jared Cox gained from being so incredibly malicious to me after he went out of his way to intentionally ruin me, even after every turn, learning I was innocent, he continued to fail to follow policy and procedure. He failed to right the ship, and get on course. Instead, he tried to bury the innocent, and was determined to make me relive the horrors of an abusive law enforcement officer. His choices have made my life a living hell, even though I'm innocent. He has some ego, and is on some kind of power trip where he thinks he can continue to ride, without consequence.

June-July 2019: Dorothea's Last Days of Freedom

On June 21, my mother called Gary in Sunset Beach to tell him that I had been arrested and that Michael and Ricky wanted to bring Dorothea, who was staying at our house, back to North Carolina. When Michael and Ricky arrived at my mother's house, she spoke to them through the storm door. Dorothea initially said, "Okay" but then told my mother she had no plans to go with them. Michael said he would be back Sunday, June 23.

That Sunday, Gary called my mother and spoke with Dorothea, who was worried about me being in jail. Dorothea stated that she wanted to go back to North Carolina and not to Florida. She warned Gary again not to give the house keys to anyone in the family.

Donna, my friend from years back, visited my mom and Dorothea on June 24 to offer support. There was a knock at the door.[6] A Baltimore County police officer had a court order to take Dorothea to the hospital for an emergency medical evaluation.

"The complaint states that Dorothea is being held captive at this address and is not taking her medication, which could cause her health to deteriorate to dangerous levels," the police officer said.

"Dorothea, do you feel you are being held captive?" Donna asked.

"No," Dorothea replied.

---

[6] This part of the story and dialogue is based on a notarized affidavit written by Donna.

Addressing the officer, Donna said, "I have witnessed Dorothea taking her medications, although she initially refused because she felt Pam's mother was hovering over her."

Dorothea angrily stated, "I do not believe I need to have a medical evaluation, officer. There is nothing wrong with me."

"I am afraid you don't have a choice, ma'am. Your nephew Michael has executed a medical power of attorney and convinced a judge to sign off on the court order," the police officer said.

With a desperate look, Dorothea glanced at Donna and my mother. Donna put her arm on Dorothea's shoulder, saying, "You better go with the officer. I will meet you at the hospital."

As they were walking out to the police car, her nephew Michael was standing in the street, and his brother David was standing near their car. On her way to the police car, Dorothea flipped them the middle finger with both hands.

At the hospital, Michael tried to get Donna thrown out, as she was not family. She admitted to the officer that it was her first-time meeting Dorothea but she had accompanied her to make sure she was okay.

"As long as you don't cause any disturbance, I cannot legally remove you. This is a public entity," the officer explained.

In the waiting room, David was sitting a few chairs down from Dorothea. "We are doing this because we love you," he said. Dorothea responded, "This is not an act of love, it is bullshit!" and stopped talking to him. When Michael came in, Dorothea refused to acknowledge him, even after he spoke to her.

After a wait, Dorothea was called for treatment. Donna had to leave, and that was the last time she was in contact with Dorothea.

That night Michael, David, and Ricky had Dorothea released from the hospital and drove through the night, back to Sunset Beach. There was never a medical report disclosed to the Assistant District Attorney and submitted to the defense as Discovery, that supported any kind of medical condition more serious than the diagnosis of the B12 deficiency. This indicates that the results of the "emergency medical evaluation" were negative with regard to Dorothea being in any immediate danger, other than possibly showing signs of agitation due to the actions/stories of Michael and Ricky which the medical staff couldn't prove one way or the other. This is also supported by the fact that they released her from the hospital the same night.

When Dorothea's former neighbor, a lawyer from Glen Arm, learned that Dorothea had been taken to the hospital for mental evaluation, she wrote the following in an email:

"While she has some memory issues, Dorothea does not appear to be incompetent in my view. Although the family appears to have a POA, this becomes only useful if Dorothea is declared incompetent."

On June 28, the family flew Dorothea to Texas for a four-day visit with Michael's children, her grandnephews, whom she had never met. According to Michael, this was done on the advice of the police in order to stay away from North Carolina. He said that Dorothea had a wonderful time but remained confused and upset.

Perhaps there was a reason Dorothea was "confused and upset." When they brought her to North Carolina from Baltimore, Maryland, she did not have any of her possessions, including her prescription medications. Her medications had been left behind at my home, because police told her they would bring her back to the house, after the medical evaluation. However, the police had lied.

Michael and Ricky returned from Texas on July 2 and said that they would stay with her around the clock "to make sure she was safe and

94

was cared for." In his letter to the court, Michael claims that during this time, I contacted Dorothea through her neighbor Gary. He told the court that Dorothea received emails and letters from me stating that I was out of jail and that I was going to go and live with her.

This is another detail in the fictional story created by Dorothea's relatives. I can swear on a stack of Bibles that at no time have I acted against the bail bond condition by contacting Dorothea after my release from jail. Check my emails, letters, texts, and phone calls ... not one, ever. I would not jeopardize my own court case by doing this. And "living with Dorothea?" I had repeatedly told her that I never had such plans and had often stated that my aging mother was my number one responsibility.

On July 3, Michael took Dorothea to a doctor's appointment. It was there that he says he learned that Dorothea's doctor at the clinic had stated that Dorothea should no longer live at home—that she must be in a facility that could take care of her because she was "a danger to herself and others." Michael insisted that they had been told the opposite by others and that this had been extremely upsetting to him and his family. Michael and Ricky stayed with Dorothea until July 8 "to make sure she was safe." The doctor filled out all the assisted living paperwork and gave Michael copies. This begs the question, AGAIN, what narrative were they telling the medical staff to get such paperwork filled out against Dorothea? They lied to police in two different states, they lied to the courts in Baltimore. Nothing had stopped them from lying. No one was listening to Dorothea deny what was happening. She was viewed as "in denial," when she was the only one telling the truth.

Her doctor had seen Dorothea on June 18. According to his report from that visit, he believed that Dorothea had some minor cognitive issues that were caused by her B12 deficiency. He gave her a B12 shot and stated that she "should not be alone so much." He advised her to see a neurologist but said that it was not urgent. That report did not say that Dorothea needed to be in a facility or was a danger to herself or others.

On July 9, Dorothea told her neighbors that the family was "taking her out for lunch." Instead, they drove her to Rosemary's house in Florida. This is the exact scenario that Dorothea described to the sheriffs in her report, that she feared that they would do to her. The next morning, they went to the assisted living facility, Inspired Living in Ocoee, Florida, enrolled Dorothea, and checked her in that afternoon.

In his letter to the court, Michael wrote that Dorothea "is now receiving three meals a day, all her medications, not drinking alcohol and has people helping her 24/7, which is what she needs."

I had no way of knowing if Dorothea was happy in her new environment because personal contact was impossible. In her petition for guardianship, Rosemary stated that Dorothea had recently made threats to harm herself if she was not discharged from the facility. These threats offer a glimpse into Dorothea's state of mind at Inspired Living. It was not "what she needed." It was not what she wanted, and it was not what she had stipulated her POA to do, when acting on her behalf. Her POA was not following her directives, but no one was listening. In Maryland, where the POA was created, not following the POA directives is a valid reason to have the POA removed from their duties.

I have visited the website of Inspired Living. It is a luxurious establishment comparable to the senior living communities here in the MD/D.C. metro area. It has all the amenities, activities, medical services, and pretty surroundings one would expect from such an institution.

Recently, however, that facility had some serious problems. Two surveys, in 2019 and 2020, by a health care agency of the state of Florida, listed a series of deficiencies at this 150-bed facility. The findings include a series of falls by clients; insufficient training for development situations; deficiencies in medication storage; self-administration of medicines; and lack of background screening of new hires. Inspired Living was penalized, at first $1,000 and later, $5,500.

Compared to the house Dorothea had lost to Rosemary in North Carolina, where she would have had her independence and the fulfillment of a retirement dream, the assisted living facility must have felt like a kind of prison.

All her civil rights have been taken away, and the family sees to it that she cannot make or receive contact from friends, co-workers, former neighbors, or acquaintances. Nobody can contact her without the permission of the court appointed guardian, Rosemary.

One can only imagine how Dorothea would be feeling if she is not experiencing dementia. She is surrounded by people she does not know and by people who might be suffering from real dementia and other illnesses. She is separated from her books, her intellectual pursuits, and her inner circle of friends. If this is not detrimental to her wellbeing and sanity, I don't know what is.

Her house in Sunset Beach has been sold, so there is no way she could return there. Her retirement dream has indeed shattered: the result of family greed, deception, and abuse, and of corruption among the people who are supposed to protect the elderly through the guardianship system.

Barely two weeks after checking Dorothea in at Inspired Living, Rosemary petitioned the court in Florida to obtain plenary guardianship for her. Rosemary also had Dorothea's health care documents changed to add a "Do Not Resuscitate" order. Dorothea had not agreed to that when she updated her legal documents. Rosemary as her POA, was making changes that Dorothea did not want, prior to Rosemary gaining control of her person and property. I will describe Rosemary's road to plenary guardianship in a later chapter.

My Quest for Justice

My mother was elated when I returned home from the North Carolina jail. This gentle nonagenarian had been worried sick about my wellbeing. By the same token, while I was in jail, my greatest worries had been about my mother being all by herself. Fortunately, our friends and neighbors had been taking care of her daily needs.

I was depressed about my failure to save Dorothea from her family's rapacity and about the injustice that they had bestowed on me. The feeling of being punched in the gut remained with me daily. I could barely eat. Tylenol did not relieve my constant headaches. The continuous sleepless nights prompted me to start drinking at one point, but even that didn't help relieve my pain.

The deep emotional stress began to affect my physical health. I tried to take care of my body by running, swimming, and biking. I couldn't go to a doctor because I could not afford medical insurance after I was fired from my jobs. Even a community clinic is $100 as you walk in the door. At one point I bought a health monitor watch so I could track these things and it would tell me if my heart rate was normal. But every time someone asked me about the case, or I was thinking in depth about it, the damn watch buzzed me with an abnormal heart rate alert.

I felt an irrepressible sense of anger at the people who were the main players: the family, the lawyers, and the police. I suffered from an overwhelming sense of hopelessness about "the System" combined with paranoia that my phone was going to be somehow wire tapped. *Was it better to be comatose? Or dead? I kept questioning, I'm a freakin' innocent "tiddlywink", why are they pursuing me?*

A thousand thoughts and questions raced through my mind. How was Dorothea coping with her forced stay at the assisted living

98

facility? How was I going to prove that my arrest had been unjust? How could I prove that I did not steal any money? To whom would I turn for help?

My friends had been supportive, but when I confided in them, they became stressed. They noticed that I was not able to move on. So, I had to internalize my anxiety and struggle alone. It was hard to go through this as a single person; I felt very alone.

A seemingly insurmountable pile of challenges was waiting for me. I had to face them for justice's sake. I had to clear myself of the charges and attempt to free Dorothea from her institutionalized "retirement."

Thank God, I kept a record of all the emails and other correspondence between Dorothea and me and with the people who had dealings with us. I needed to gather all the official records on my case, organize them, and copy them. And I needed legal advice, so I hired a North Carolina attorney to represent me.[7]

I had very little experience with lawyers. Now I needed lawyers to help with efforts to work on Dorothea's behalf. It was so very frustrating. No one wanted to reach out to help Dorothea. I had all the evidence to prove Rosemary was lying about everything. I had to get it to Dorothea to help her, but no one would help. I had the restraining order on me, so I couldn't do it myself. I was devastated. I was a failure. Everyone told me I had to clear my name first and then help Dorothea. That didn't sit well with me. She had no one working to help her.

Something inside just told me that I had to be careful when talking to lawyers. Of course, by law they must represent their clients'

---

[7] This dialogue between my lawyer and me is based on the Felony Prosecution Report that led to my arrest in Baltimore, MD, on June 20, 2019.

interests, but that does not always happen. Their positions in "the System" might color the way they defend a client because they want to maintain these positions. After all, they are not gods; they are just

human beings. And the court is the daily playing field that they must return to "fight" each day. They fight the same people; they merely change their team players, but their front office remains the same. Winks and nods are a routine. Some good ones will work with you. The bad ones only want a check and work as little as possible. That boils down to minimalistic plea bargain lawyers.

On Saturday evening, Gary drove me to the North Carolina lawyer that Dorothea's neighbor had arranged for me. He reviewed the charging documents and told me what to expect on Monday in court.

This lawyer seemed somewhat annoyed by my reactions to the charges and indifferent to what had really transpired over the last month. I felt that he was not interested in my responses to the charges. Although I did not have any documentation with me to refute the charges, I wanted him to know that I had studied my accusers' statements very well. I told him outright, "I don't want you to make up stuff or embellish anything. You need to ask me questions, so I can tell you what actually happened, where to get the evidence and who has it, i.e. witness names, statements and actions." My lawyer replied, "Let's review their claims."

- *They say you claimed to be a former student, but Dorothea didn't know you.*
- *They claim they hired a realtor; packed the Glen Arm home, including Rosemary's childhood memorabilia; they hired the mover; they held an estate sale; and, they drove Dorothea to NC.*
- *They claim you rifled through the boxes they moved to North Carolina and only 9 of 25 boxes remained.*
- *They told the police they were concerned about your secrecy and intentions, so Rosemary had her name placed on Dorothea's bank accounts. She claims that while she was looking at the bank accounts, $125K disappeared.*

100

- *They claim that they called Fidelity to lock down the financial accounts, and that Fidelity asked Rosemary to be the Power of Attorney on record.*
- *Detective Cox claims that Baltimore County Police told him you were not a sworn officer, but maybe a volunteer crossing guard.*
- *Detective Cox also claimed that Michael told him they were traveling to Maryland to see the lawyer and get a certified copy of the POA.*

I explained how each of these convoluted claims were false, but this lawyer merely suggested I not speak to anyone else about the case. He then suggested I give passwords and IDs to Dorothea's family. Oddly enough, emails between Det. Cox and Michael detail that Detective Cox had already listened to the jail cell phone calls between my mom and me, and when he learned the Passwords and IDs, he himself gave them to Michael. *Is that even legal?* The bank wouldn't even give Michael or Rosemary access to the accounts, because they lacked a certified POA.

My lawyer refused to obtain bank statements and witness testimony. *Why, I don't' know.* When I demanded to know what his plan of action was, he suggested I hire a new attorney, and he promptly filed a motion to the court to withdraw from the case. I was devastated. All the accusations could easily be proven to be false, but this lawyer didn't care to defend me, an innocent person.

Now I had the task of trying to find another attorney to defend me. Exploitation of the Elderly is a horrific crime, and no one wanted to take the case and defend me. No one believed in my innocence. Exploitation has become such a common place crime, that it's viewed as a "slam dunk" in the courts. There is no "innocent before proven guilty." If I recall correctly, at my first court hearing, even the North Carolina judge said, "Your client should know, we take elder abuse very seriously here." I wish they took investigation and evidence very seriously, too.

It took nearly two weeks before I was able to find another North Carolina attorney to take my case. As a non-resident of North Carolina, I was at a disadvantage. I had never ventured out beyond Dorothea's immediate neighborhood, so I was unfamiliar with the proximity of the various counties to the courthouse. I didn't have friends in the area for lawyer recommendations. So, I had no referrals on which I could rely. Navigating from out of state was very difficult. Every phone call or email required me to keep repeating the humiliating charges against me, and begging them to believe me took its toll on my confidence.

My relationship with my new lawyer lasted a little longer, only because I was in fear he would also withdraw from the case. To my chagrin and shock, this lawyer also refused to obtain bank statements, and interview any witnesses. He claimed that was not his responsibility but the responsibility of the ADA.

He would repeatedly and strongly suggest that I take the plea bargains offered by the Assistant District Attorney. These plea bargains required me to pay money (that I never stole) to the family who was lying about me. The ADA presented these plea bargains without having the bank statements, (that proved no money was missing), and threatened me with an indictment if I didn't take the plea bargain. Sure enough, I was indicted without any evidence, even though evidence was readily available.

The plea deal stated that I would repay stolen money and plead guilty to Exploitation of the Trust of a Disabled Elder. The State recommended a conditional discharge with the following conditions: 36 months of supervised probation; 24 hours of community service; no contact with Dorothea; regular employment; and, any other terms and conditions imposed by the court.

If I accepted a plea deal, I was saying that I admit guilt. However, my lawyer framed it as if I would merely acknowledge that the ADA probably didn't have enough evidence to find me guilty in court. Additionally, I'd give up rights to a trial by jury and couldn't file an appeal.

Further, this would stay on my record until eligible for expungement, thereby affecting any attempts at employment, earning potential and other aspects of my life. My lawyer tried to tell me that I wouldn't have to tell future employers of the felony charges. Keep in mind, I was working in law enforcement, when the accusations were made, and the accusations were the reason for my termination. *How would I be expected to explain years of unemployment to a future employer, or answer a polygraph question as required for employment with a law enforcement agency?* His explanation didn't sit well with me. It was clear to me that he didn't have experience in this area. Rather than pursuing justice, bad law enforcement tends to rely on the prosecution making deals, and details of the case become less important to them.

This is what happened in my case. My lawyer presented the plea bargain as more favorable because, a jury trial would be more time consuming and costly to prepare. This told me to he was not engaged in my case or not experienced enough to prepare for my trial. The original charges that Rosemary and her family made to police were never properly investigated and were accepted at face value by the guardianship courts in Florida. With this being the case, I terminated my second attorney's services.

I now needed a new lawyer who would work for dismissal of all charges. With the help of my brother and his friends, we found incredibly competent attorney's in another county in North Carolina. This legal team came with a hefty price tag. However, they did what the others refused to do — they went to work.

My new legal team gathered witnesses who testified that in all my former caregiver roles, there was never any neglect or abuse. Another witness testified that I never attempted to become Dorothea's POA. The bank records showed that at no time did money go missing nor was any money ever misappropriated by me.

My lawyers had serious issues with the lack of police investigation into my charges. I was never interviewed. Had they witnesses, they'd have learned: that I never "posed as a student;" I never lived with Dorothea nor promised to live with her; Dorothea's neighbors and friends thought she was competent to remain in her house; Dorothea told everyone that her sister was trying to place her in an assisted living facility and she did not want to go; I believed the security camera videos captured elder abuse by Rosemary and her family, and that I was trying to alert police and other government authorities of the progression of these events. Despite this, the police adopted the family's incomplete and untrue statements without conducting a serious investigation of their allegations against me.

My new legal team would attempt to prove that I never should have been subjected to the egregious charges of abuse and exploitation. I could only hope that this would lead to the dismissal of all the charges against me.

This might be the right moment to introduce some information about the guardianship system's history and inner workings. I'll do so in the next chapter.

Guardianships: Good or Evil?

In the almost three years I have been involved in this case, I have learned a lot about guardianship in the U.S. legal system. After spending time in jail and attempting to prove my innocence, I also learned more about lawyers, courts, and law enforcement than I had ever wanted to know.

Before describing how Rosemary and her family manipulated the system to gain guardianship over Dorothea, I want to share some of the insights I gained into the guardianship system.

I hope that all these legal and historical details will not bore you, but will enlighten you. If you want to understand what happened to Dorothea, you need to know how the guardianship system operates and how it is able to put people into institutions against their will.

The idea of guardianship — that is, one person being responsible for another — is very old. The ancient Greeks had laws that governed property and inheritance. The Roman Republic developed the idea of *parens patriae* (parent of the fatherland), meaning that the state had the power to act as guardian for those who were unable to take care of themselves. In 449 B.C., the Law of the Twelve Tables *(Leges duodecim tabularum)* established the care of children, women, and people who were considered "insane." The Roman Empire adopted these laws and made guardianship a public office.

During the Middle Ages, the feudal system and the church made the Roman system their own. In medieval England the task was handed over to the Courts of Chancery to prevent properties from going to the church. In operation from 1280 to 1852, the Courts of Chancery functioned as courts of equity — courts tasked with determining "what is fair" as opposed to "what is legal" in a court of law.

With the development of the medical establishment in the 1800s, medical staff got involved with the guardianship system; they evaluated who was impaired. In the United Kingdom, the doctors were called to help determine who was impaired throughout the 1900s.

The young United States of America placed the responsibility of adult guardianship into the hands of the individual states. Over time, most of the states assigned guardianship procedures to their probate courts, which handled wills and estates of the dead. They all developed statutes based on inherited principles and their own situations.

After this short history of guardianship, you might be thinking: Is it not wonderful that our nation has a legal system that takes care of people who cannot take care of themselves anymore? The state protects children who are neglected by their parents. The state also assigns responsible people who volunteer to make sure that their relatives are well cared for and handle their finances when they are found too old to do it themselves or when they are struck by dementia or other ailments. Is this not a blessing for the estimated 52 million Americans in 2020 who had reached sixty-five and older?

Since my arrest in June 2019, I have been dealing with America's guardianship courts—the courts of equity—and with the courts of law. And there are snakes in the grass.

In a court of law, the "letter of the law" is the guiding principle. There is due process; there are rules of evidence and the constitutional right to a trial by jury. One can only hope that the three principal court standards of proof are adhered to: reasonable doubt, clear and convincing evidence, and preponderance of the evidence. I will share my experience with these courts later.

In a court of equity, where the guiding principle is "what is fair," it is the judge's perception of what is equitable, fair, and equal

that counts the most. No juries are allowed. The judge decides what evidence to admit, whom to believe, and what statutes are applicable. It's up to the judge to select which witnesses to hear and to determine the boundaries of fairness.

Dr. Sam Sugar, founder of the organization Americans Against Abusive Probate Guardianship, states it best in his book *Guardianships and the Elderly: The Perfect Crime*. In probate court, "A judge has complete latitude to establish a guardianship based solely on his assessment of the 'facts' of a case as presented by a court insider, even if there has been no investigation of the allegations that precipitated the case."[8]

Dr. Sugar points to other issues with probate courts. [9] Many states lack comprehensive recordkeeping, which makes it almost impossible to know how many people are under guardianship. Political influence can raise its ugly head because most probate judges are elected, not appointed. Although every state has its statutes, they are often superseded by so-called "probate rules" developed by attorneys over time and widely accepted by the courts.

An array of people is involved in the guardianship process. They all contribute in their own way to having the court declare an allegedly incapacitated person (AIP), or "Ward." The Ward is then stripped of all civil rights. The petitioners initiate the evaluation process when they deem persons to be incapacitated, to be a danger to themselves, or to be in danger of being abused. Usually, the petitioners are family members. They

---

[8] Dr. Sam Sugar, *Guardianships and the Elderly. The Perfect Crime.* New York: Square One Publishers, 2018, p. 34.

[9] Dr. Sugar has graciously granted me permission to use the materials from his work which I have used.

can invoke the help of law enforcement to serve court orders or to apprehend people who are suspected to be a danger to themselves.

The guardian must undergo a criminal history check, attend a short educational course, and put up a bond if the Ward's assets are

considerable. Often the guardian is given limited guardianship for a certain period of time. This usually leads to plenary guardianship, granting rights to handle all legal decisions on behalf of the Ward.

Then there are the court-appointed attorneys. Their task is to make sure Wards understand their rights and the consequences of guardianship. They must examine the evidence, secure testimony, and make sure that the Ward's rights are protected.

After examining all the evidence, the judges are responsible for creating the guardianship. They approve fees for lawyers and guardians and monitor guardians' activities after they obtain guardianship.

Finally, there are the examining committees. They are the people who furnish evidence of incapacity. At least one member of this committee has to be a medical doctor. Judges can accept or reject their recommendations. At the fringes of this whole process are other people who might play a role: social workers, caregivers, financial advisors, estate handlers, and so on.

All the players in these proceedings enjoy judicial immunity, meaning they cannot be sued except for egregious violations of ethics or rules.

All these people are paid for their services, either during the court case or after guardianship has been granted. These payments are usually taken from the Ward's assets. No wonder then that the entire system became a moneymaking business that is protected from the inside.

I again have to agree with Dr. Sugar, who states: "Absent meaningful supervision or monitoring, the penultimate power of the probate judge can and often does succumb to the forces that pollute the equity process and result in unnecessary and fraudulent guardianships and all that they entail."[10]

To initiate guardianship, it must be determined if the "incapacitated person" is indeed incapacitated. Once that has been established, the process of appointing a guardian can begin.

I should note here that during most guardianship proceedings in court, the individual who supposedly needs the care is not even present. In Dorothea's case, no judge has ever seen or met her, or had a chance to personally evaluate her comportment.

In most states, the statutes require courts to investigate whether there are less restrictive alternatives to guardianship. Dorothea's lawyer attempted such an approach, claiming that an existing POA and health care proxy would be less restrictive. His attempts were dismissed by the court.

Finally, there are reported cases where courts did not sufficiently screen petitioners ahead of time and allowed guardians to profit from their guardianship. Some refer to these cases as "legal kidnappings."

Case in point: In my defense against the abuse charges, my attorneys stated that, after discovery, it became clear that some of Rosemary's allegations of wrongdoing were "verifiably false." I will describe the details later in the story. It is clear, however, that the courts accepted Rosemary's allegations without sufficient investigation of the police reports.

What happens after the guardianship has been ordered?

---

[10] Ibid., p. 41.

Once given plenary guardianship, the guardian has absolute control over all aspects of the Ward's life. I have already described in detail the powers Rosemary and her family gained by obtaining guardianship. I just want to add a couple of things that are sometimes surprising to the Ward once they have been placed in an assisted living facility.

According to Dr. Sugar, "Even if the Ward has legally set forth her wishes for end-of-life care and inheritance distribution prior to the establishment of the guardianship, those documents are no longer enforceable under the rules of the guardianship."[11] This means that the Wards have no control over who their doctors are or what medications they take. In Dorothea's case, the letter she wrote expressing her desire to fully retire at Sunset Beach and use home care if needed became moot under the rules of guardianship.

There are, however, other models of guardianship.[12] One is the least restrictive alternative model. In this type of guardianship, the guardian must select the model that is least restrictive of the Ward's freedom and independence and must give the Ward a chance to participate in making decisions.

Another model is the substituted judgment model. In this type of guardianship, guardians must make decisions that the Wards would have made if they still had capacity. Under this approach, the Ward's prior expressed wishes and personal values are important factors to be considered.

From Rosemary's petition and the family's efforts to prove that Dorothea was suffering from dementia, it does not look as if they considered these alternative guardianships at all. They went for the most comprehensive setup.

---

[11] Ibid., p. 3.

[12] See "Guardianship," Encyclopedia.com, updated May 21, 2018.

One can only speculate what kind of choices Dorothea would have made if she could have participated in the decision making. Would she have chosen an assisted living facility in Florida? Or would she have preferred a facility in Baltimore, MD where she would have been surrounded by familiar faces? Would she have consented to being unable to contact her friends or be contacted by them without the permission of the guardians or their lawyers? Would she have insisted on her wishes to spend her last days in Sunset Beach and be assisted by caregivers if needed, as she had expressed in a signed letter before the family took her to Florida?

Keep in mind that guardianships are not necessarily lifelong situations. Many adult guardianships continue for the Ward's lifetime and are terminated only by death. But what if the Ward recovers, in whole or in part? What if it is established that Dorothea's memory problems were exclusively caused by her B12 deficiency and not by dementia? What if she has learned to take care of herself again, as she did for so many years? What if there are other circumstances that suggest that her guardianship is no longer needed?

In all states, a Ward may request termination of the guardianship. This can happen in a formal petition or can be made by an informal letter. In some cases, the Ward might be supported by family members who have questioned the petition. In a contested guardianship, it is difficult for them to reverse the court decision because they are prevented from communicating directly with the Ward and can do so only with the permission of the guardians and their lawyers. The court might even issue a stay away order.

To conclude this section, I want to add some thoughts on incapacity. Let us, for a moment, try to enter Dorothea's mind. All the plans she had to retire in her home in Sunset Beach have been completely changed without her permission. She has no control anymore over anything she owns: it is all in the hands of her sister and her relatives. She is living in a facility that others chose for her, where she is medicated by doctors she did not choose. Her sister decides whom she can contact and who can contact her. She is shut off from her friends and former colleagues.

Before "incapacity," the term used in guardianship cases was "incompetence." An incompetent person was someone who could not take responsibility for decisions and actions. Over time, the courts chose the less restrictive term "incapacity." That term covers a wide range of issues, from slight memory loss to total dementia and other mental ailments, including coma. I already mentioned that this is a legal term, not a medical one. Doctors' opinions are rarely viewed as important, except when they come from an examining committee.

How does an examining board work? Its members, headed by a physician, must take a three-to-four-hour instructional course and may be paid up to $400 per hour to serve. Not exactly the necessary academic background to judge someone's mental capacity! This group then goes through a brief check-the-box evaluation of the person and relays the results to the judge. These evaluations can be based on unproven testimony provided to the committee. The judge is also able to disallow any evidence contrary to the findings of the group.

If the judge thinks that this is an emergency situation, the judge can order temporary guardianship for a period of 90 to 180 days. This temporary solution usually leads to plenary guardianship later. This is exactly what happened in Dorothea's case.

One could question whether probate courts are applying enough transparency and fairness, enough due process of law, to safeguard every citizen's life, liberty, and property as defined in the U.S. Constitution's fourteenth amendment: "No State shall make or enforce any law which shall abridge the privileges or immunities of citizens of the United States; nor shall any State deprive any person of life, liberty, or property, without due process of law; nor deny to any person within its jurisdiction the equal protection of the laws." It might explain why sixty percent of abusive guardianships were initiated by an emergency temporary guardianship.

Now that I have enriched your knowledge about guardianships, it is time to come to some conclusions. I am inspired by Dr. Sugar's conclusions and might add some conclusions myself.[13]

It is increasingly clear that the guardianship system is running amok. State statutes are always subject to federal law, but that seems not to be the case when it comes to guardianship and inheritance matters. The judges in the probate system are incredibly powerful, and one cannot appeal to a federal court or the Justice Department in case of disagreement. These judges don't have to listen to a panel of their peers, because in the equity courts system there are no juries.

Several things need to happen to rein in the power of these courts. Breaking the ring of silence around the proceedings could be a first step: the concealment and sequestration of the proceedings should end. As a Catholic, this silence from the courts to protect their power reminds me of my church's problems with pedophilia. The bishops were silent and were hiding their priests' crimes against children just to protect their clerical power.

The capacity examination system needs a serious overhaul. Not only should examiners be better educated but judges should allow evidence that counters the examiners' evaluations.

Before receiving plenary guardianship, guardians should be required to consider alternative models of guardianship. In general, the least restrictive measures should have absolute priority.

---

[13] Sugar, op. cit., pp. 199-203.

The states should set up criminal complaint departments where abuse and exploitation can be examined before the case goes to probate court.

There should be more stringent investigations of the allegations made by petitioners, and evidence contrary to the allegations should be part of the petition. It would also help if there were stringent caps on legal fees.

Advance health directives are usually abrogated in a guardianship. The Ward made these directives when in a responsible state of mind. Guardianship should not take away the right to decide what happens with your health care when you are unable to make these decisions.

For almost two centuries, state legislators made statutes and judges made decisions that served their self-interest and greed. By not allowing their proceedings to be made public and with minimal oversight from the outside, they kept a low profile. As a result, millions of Wards were taken advantage of by courts, guardians, and associates. It is indeed a system in disarray, and it needs to be replaced by something better.

There have been attempts to alert the public to problems with the guardianship system. In 1987, the Associated Press reviewed more than 2,000 cases and published a report, "Guardians of the Elderly: An Ailing System." In 1988 the U.S. House Committee on Aging had a hearing that was followed by a National Guardianship Symposium. They made 31 recommendations for improvement of the system, especially for professional guardians; among them was the need to license, register, and certify guardians. The symposium had follow-up sessions in 2001, 2004, and 2011. Although some states made modest changes based on some of these recommendations, in general the courts kept acting as "courts of equity" and circumvented some of their own state laws.

In October 2017, President Donald J. Trump signed the Elder Protection and Prosecution Act. Its purpose was to increase the federal

114

government's focus on preventing elder abuse and exploitation. The Justice Department followed up with the Elder Justice Initiative, participating in criminal and civil enforcement actions involving misconduct that targeted vulnerable seniors. It also established a National Elder Fraud Hotline where people can report elder abuse: 1-833-372- 8311. Despite this first-of-its-kind federal

intervention, many of the state courts that handle guardianships continued with their old customs and practices. Dorothea's guardianship is a case in point.

In 2018, the U.S. Senate Commission on Aging, under the chairmanship of Sen. Susan Collins, issued a report on guardianships. According to the Executive Summary, "Unscrupulous guardians acting with little oversight have used guardianship proceedings to obtain control of vulnerable individuals and have then used that control to liquidate liquid assets and savings for their own personal benefit." The commission recognizes that all states have laws designed to protect due process but believes that these laws are not always consistently enforced. The commission explains that more must be done to protect individuals subject to guardianship.

The committee then provides some advice for improving the guardianship system. It recommends that guardians undergo criminal background checks; that courts and federal agencies collaborate better; that a volunteer program be initiated of individuals who can help inform the court about the possible Ward before guardianship is given and periodically throughout the guardianship; and that all parties related to the guardianship be better trained on guardian responsibilities and signs of abuse.

The report encourages the use of less restrictive alternatives and promotes the restoration of the Ward's rights. To accomplish this, the committee recommends that less restrictive alternatives, limited guardianships, and supported decision making be promoted. There should be increased comprehensive training and education of all officials and guardians to spot opportunities for restoration of a Ward's rights when it becomes appropriate. State laws need to be strengthened to ensure that individuals seeking a restoration get legal representation and access to resources. Finally, the report recommends greater uniformity in the state guardianship laws and suggests nationwide adoption of uniform guardianship.

In summary, there are three key areas that should be addressed to protect the well-being of individuals placed under guardianship. First, the oversight of guardians and guardianship arrangements should be increased. There are few safeguards in place to protect against individuals who choose to abuse the system. Greater oversight would protect against abuse, neglect, and exploitation.

Second, full guardianship might not always be the best means of providing protection to an individual. If and when an individual regains capacity, all or some rights should be restored. As the committee asserts, "Unfortunately, this rarely occurs."

Third, there is a need for better data. Few states are able to report accurate or detailed guardianship data. The numbers of individuals under guardianship are largely unavailable.

Despite these noble efforts by the federal government in the last few years, not many states have acted upon the recommendations. I cannot help but think that, if the state guardianship systems in North Carolina and Florida had implemented the recommendations of the 2018 Senate committee, Dorothea would presently be enjoying her retirement in Sunset Beach.

How exactly did Rosemary and her family obtain plenary guardianship over Dorothea? This chapter will address that. The details are collected from Rosemary's official petitions to the court and the court's responses. They are in the public domain.

An analysis of Rosemary's petitions is important because there are provably false allegations, inaccuracies, and even plain inventions. Even more important, the Florida court accepted Rosemary's allegations at face value when giving her the guardianship. The family's allegations appeared earlier in this story, but they warrant repetition in the context of this new petition for plenary guardianship.

After Rosemary and Michael had been assigned as POAs in 2017, and she had almost doubled her inheritance by changing Dorothea's will, she and her family were ready in 2019 to go for plenary guardianship. They would do anything to make sure that Dorothea became their Ward and was safely stowed away in an assisted living facility. The story will show how they misrepresented facts, manufactured allegations, and made me the villain who was after Dorothea's possessions. The police and the courts swallowed their arguments whole, and the family succeeded.

Reviewing these court documents made my blood boil, but I will not comment on the veracity of her arguments. You will be the judge.

In the middle of July 2019, a week after Dorothea had been registered at Inspired Living, Rosemary signed a statement that she would submit to a criminal history background screening and attend the Guardian Education Course in Florida within four months of being appointed to serve as guardian.

A week later she filed a Petition for Appointment of Guardian at the probate division of a circuit court in Florida.

In this petition Rosemary cited all the reasons why guardianship was necessary for Dorothea and why she was the right person to serve as guardian.

Rosemary stated that Dorothea (the Ward) was an alleged incapacitated person who had been diagnosed with "dementia, cognitive dysfunction, altered mental status, and confusion." She filed medical records and doctors' reports finding that "Dorothea was unable to live independently and needed supervision and assistance with the functional activities of daily living, including assistance in the management of her personal and financial affairs." Rosemary stated that doctors and medical professionals treating Dorothea had recommended placement in an assistant living facility for her safety and protection.

Rosemary further stated that there was an ongoing investigation pending before a North Carolina court involving elder abuse and exploitation of Dorothea by me, a former acquaintance.

As petitioner, she further alleged that in 2017, following the death of Dorothea's long-time partner, I befriended Dorothea, posing as a former student, and subsequently exploited her deficits and gained access to her bank accounts and property, resulting in at least $125,000 to $150,000 being taken from Dorothea.

Rosemary asserted that I moved in with Dorothea approximately three months after we first met and thereafter took steps to isolate her from family and friends. Rosemary alleged that I placed cameras throughout Dorothea's home, including her bathroom and bedroom, and refused to provide information and access to Rosemary, Dorothea's half-sister and POA.

She also contended that I contacted Dorothea's investment advisor's attorney and tried to have myself added to Dorothea's accounts and appointed as her POA in place of Rosemary. She further claimed that I attempted to have an order of protection issued against her on behalf of Dorothea in order to further isolate her from her sister.

Rosemary stated that I was arrested on or about June 27, 2019, for elder abuse and exploitation of Dorothea. (Exhibit A contains copies of news articles and court records.)[14]

She maintained that recorded jailhouse phone records revealed that I had changed all the passwords for online access to Dorothea's bank accounts and was recorded giving these passwords to a third person on the phone.

Rosemary claimed that, since my release on bond, I had written letters and attempted to contact Dorothea.

Following my arrest, Rosemary had filed guardianship proceedings with the state of North Carolina for the protection of Dorothea and her real property located within that state. However, such proceedings were dismissed upon the advice of North Carolina counsel since Dorothea was physically present in Florida, and North Carolina would not require ancillary proceedings for Dorothea's real property. Moreover, Rosemary believed that it would be detrimental to Dorothea's mental health and wellbeing to be returned to North Carolina for any court hearing.

Rosemary stated that she was currently serving as attorney-in-fact and agent for her sister, pursuant to a Baltimore, MD statuary form Limited Power of Attorney for Dorothea of June 2017.[15]

---

[14] In mentioning exhibits, we only give a short description, not the actual content.

[15] In June 2019 Rosemary paid a $20 recording fee and a total of $67 to Baltimore Maryland. Three days later—that is, two years after its creation—the Circuit Court of Baltimore County certified a copy of the original POA of June 2017. The document, prepared by two lawyers in Baltimore, bears Dorothea's signature and is signed by a

Rosemary was also serving as health care surrogate for Dorothea under that Advanced Health Care Directive of June 2017. Based on the unique circumstances of this case, Rosemary stated that she did not believe that the POA and health care surrogate were less restrictive alternatives to the appointment of a guardian for Dorothea. Rosemary did not believe that her sister was able to understand and appreciate the nature and the extent of her limitations and thus was susceptible to undue influence and exploitation, which she said had already occurred. She alleged that Dorothea was resistant to receiving support and assistance, notwithstanding the findings of her doctors that she needed such support. She noted that Dorothea struggled to maintain proper hygiene and often failed or refused to take her medication as prescribed.

She stated that Dorothea had a history of alcohol abuse and had recently threatened to harm herself if she was not discharged from her current facility. Rosemary reported that she was working through these issues with Dorothea and her treatment team.

The petition then stated that Rosemary was not a professional guardian but that, as the Ward's sister, she was *sui juris* and otherwise qualified under the laws of Florida to act as Guardian of the Person and Property of the Ward. According to the petition, the proposed guardian should be appointed because she was familiar with Dorothea's physical, mental, emotional, and financial care needs and was willing to serve to ensure that her sister was protected from physical danger or harm, and that her property was secured and not subject to misappropriation.

Then followed a list of the property subject to the guardianship: the house in North Carolina, cash and investments, and tangible property, totaling close to $2,000,000. She included a

---

notary, followed by his seal, and is witnessed by Dorothea's lawyer. All pages of the deed were registered in North Carolina in May 2021.

"potential claim and/or cause of action against" me with unknown value.

Concluding the petition, Rosemary stated that this guardianship of the person and property was being sought in good faith for Dorothea for her protection and for her physical, mental, emotional, and financial well-being; and for financial accountability purposes and continuity of care during her lifetime, which would be in her best interest and in accordance with her wishes.

Rosemary declared that under penalty of perjury, she had read the foregoing, and that the facts alleged were true to the best of her knowledge and belief.

Dorothea's brother Ricky, his sons, Michael and David, and a daughter of Rosemary were notified that they had to sign a consent to the Petition to Determine Capacity, Petition for Appointment of Emergency Temporary Guardian, and Petition for Appointment of Guardian for Rosemary.

In mid-August, a circuit judge of the probate division of a Florida County Circuit Court ordered the appointment of Rosemary as emergency temporary guardian of Dorothea. The judge stated that it appeared that "there was an imminent danger that the physical or mental health or safety of the alleged incapacitated person will be seriously impaired or that the property of that person is in danger of being wasted, misappropriated or lost unless immediate action is taken." Rosemary stated that she was qualified to serve and was appointed as Dorothea's emergency temporary guardian for 90 days, until mid-November 2019.

At this same hearing, the judge signed Letters of Emergency Temporary Guardianship of Person and Property and declared Rosemary the temporary guardian. Her powers and duties were subsequently described:

- to marshal, protect, secure, and preserve all assets

- to set up a guardianship account where the guardian can receive income on behalf of the Ward as well as pay and account for all reasonable expenses of the Ward and those for the protection of the Ward

- to make all medical, residential, travel, and social decisions for the Ward, including the review of medical records

- to move for Ward with the elder abuse and exploitation claim in progress in North Carolina.

At the end of the order, the judge mentioned that there was a Limited Power of Attorney and Health Care Surrogate in existence naming Rosemary (the POA of June 2017).

In mid-November 2019 the judge extended Rosemary's temporary guardianship until mid-February 2020. (The powers and duties of the guardianship described above were repeated.)

Dorothea's court-appointed lawyer filed a Memorandum of Law with the court asking that no temporary guardianship be given to Rosemary.

He claimed that Dorothea's fundamental right to privacy protected her power to make decisions concerning her person and property. According to Florida law, the court was required to use the least intrusive form of assistance. Upon a finding of incapacity, the court was required to appoint a guardian unless there was a less restrictive alternative to guardianship. It was within the power of the court to find someone incapacitated yet not appoint a guardian.

The attorney argued that Dorothea had executed a Limited Power of Attorney and an Advanced Health Care Directive in June 2017, giving Rosemary the power to act as her agent.

That POA would address Dorothea's needs and should be given priority over statutory guardianship, he asserted. If permanent guardianship was assigned, this POA would have to be suspended, and that had not yet happened. Therefore, the original POA remained valid. The durable POA took priority over any guardianship proceedings. In these circumstances, appointing a guardian served no purpose and should be denied, he contended. It would further impinge upon Dorothea's right of privacy.

Should the court determine that a guardian was in Dorothea's best interest, Rosemary should be appointed as sole plenary guardian of Dorothea's person and property under the durable POA and health care power of June 2017.

Dorothea's attorney's plea was dismissed. Towards the end of November 2019, the court ordered the appointment of Rosemary as plenary guardian. The court found that the Ward was totally incapacitated and that it was necessary for a plenary guardian to be appointed.

Rosemary was now qualified to serve and was appointed. She had to take the prescribed oath and enter a bond to the state of Florida. She had to place the Fidelity Investments brokerage accounts in a restricted account in a financial institution. The limited POA was superseded, and the guardian could now exercise all the rights assigned to the POA and health care surrogate. The court stated that the guardian would be responsible for all personal, medical, social, travel, residential, and health care decisions for the Ward. There was a handwritten note added that read, "subject to the intent expressed previously by Ward in her Advanced Health Care Directive dated June 2017." The bond was paid in December to a local insurance company.

The Letter of Plenary Guardianship, signed that same day, states that the plenary guardian "will have due power to have the care, custody and control of the Ward, to exercise all delegable rights and

123

powers of the Ward, to administer the property of the Ward according to the law, and to take possession of and hold, for the benefit of the Ward, all the property and income of the Ward."

In mid-February 2020, the circuit court wrote a statement that Rosemary had filed an initial guardianship report about Dorothea's physical and mental health care, personal and social services, residential setting, insurance, verified inventory, and audit fee in a timely manner.

A week later Rosemary, through her lawyer, stated that it would be in Dorothea's best interest to dispense with the requirement of a depository and to instead have her assets remain at Fidelity Investments so that the funds could remain invested. Rosemary could pay Dorothea's bills and expenses as her needs fluctuated, and account for such payments to the court. Rosemary was willing and able to post a bond for the full amount of the assets, as required by the Florida statutes.

During the last week of January 2020 Rosemary filed her "Guardian's Verified Inventory" in court, listing Dorothea's total cash and investment assets, including retirement accounts and an annuity. She also listed Dorothea's monthly income from Social Security and her pension.

In early March 2020, a circuit judge approved the initial guardianship report and stated that the report met the Ward's needs. He authorized the guardian to act only in areas in which the Ward had been declared incapacitated. He gave her the authority to serve as guardian for the forthcoming year. That same day he ordered the motion to increase the bond in lieu of establishing a depository. The bond had to be posted by mid-March 2020. In the Amended Order on the same day, he added that none of the property was to be placed in a restricted account in a financial institution. He also stated that the Ward's limited POA was superseded.

A paragraph of the November order was repeated: "The guardian shall be responsible for all personal, medical, social, travel, residential and health care decisions for the Ward, subject to the intent expressed previously by Ward in her Advanced Health Care Directive of June 2017. There would be no withdrawals without court approval."

At the end of May 2020, Rosemary petitioned the court to sell the Chevrolet Dorothea had bought to replace her Honda SUV. Rosemary stated that Dorothea was unable to drive and her license had been revoked. She wanted the proceeds "to be used for Dorothea's care and benefit." The judge authorized the sale.

Rosemary then petitioned the court to authorize her to list and sell Dorothea's home in Sunset Beach. She alleged that Dorothea suffered from "dementia, cognitive dysfunction, altered mental status, and confusion." Based on Dorothea's condition and diagnosis, "the guardian does not believe that the Ward will be able to live independently"; as a result, this property was no longer of use to the Ward, and it was an ongoing expense to the guardianship. Rosemary proposed a list price of $590,000 for the property "as is." The proceeds of this sale would be deposited into the guardianship to provide additional funds for the Ward's ongoing care.

The court ordered the authorization in October 2020 by giving Rosemary the exclusive right to list and sell the property and to deposit the proceeds into the guardianship. The house was sold for approximately $560,000 later that year.

In late February 2021, Rosemary's lawyer filed a motion with the court in Florida to extend the deadline for filing her annual guardianship report. She said that would need additional time to "gather information from the Ward's medical providers and financial institution to include in the Annual Report." The motion was granted.

In early March 2021, Rosemary petitioned the court three times to reimburse expenses for Dorothea's benefit incurred by Ricky, Michael, and herself. She stated that each had expended their own funds and that each was "helping secure the Ward's property in North Carolina, to pursue an elder exploitation claim against Pam in North Carolina, and help the Ward and her property move to the facility in Florida where the Ward now resides." In each separate petition, she claimed that without this help and assistance "the Ward's person and property could have been subjected to further exploitation by Pam." The total reimbursement requested was thousands and thousands of dollars. They provided the court with bank statements and credit card records showing their costs for travel, hotels, meals, court costs, and copying, among other items.

Since moving Dorothea into Inspired Living, Rosemary has been very busy securing control over her sister's life. Between the day Rosemary filed her petition for temporary guardianship and her request for reimbursement of costs in March 2021, there was a steady flow of court petitions that led to Rosemary's plenary guardianship and its associated activities. The courts consistently approved Rosemary's petitions.

In the meantime, Dorothea had been at the assisted living facility for 20 months, unable to make any decisions about her health or finances. She had lost her retirement dream house in North Carolina and had been deprived of all her civil rights. Next to my feelings about the injustice that had been done to me by jailing me, I felt that even a greater injustice had been done to Dorothea.

There is no way to know how Dorothea feels about all of this. One would have to go through her family's lawyers to talk to Dorothea or even to obtain information from secondhand sources. The only assurance that she is okay and receives all the physical and medical care she needs as a "person with dementia" comes from statements by the family.

There are some "what-ifs" to be considered in this case. What if Dorothea's memory problems are purely related to her B12 deficiency and not to dementia? What if her issues with social interactions are merely symptoms of her character? What if the charges of me stealing from Dorothea, which were used to obtain guardianship, are proven to be fallacious? What if it becomes clear that the family showed concern for Dorothea only after she lost her lifelong friend and was alone in the world?

I need to add a couple of final comments. The petition for reimbursement of the family's expenses for Dorothea's care illustrates an interesting aspect of the story. The letters of Ricky and Michael are full of expressions of concern and love for their Aunt Dorothea. Rosemary's guardianship petitions time and again say that everything is being done for Dorothea's benefit and safety. Megan once said to Dorothea, "You look sad . . . but Mom is doing this for you." And David: "We are doing this because we love you."

But once Dorothea was "safe" at the assisted living facility, they kept all receipts and highlighted bank records of the expenses they made for "dear auntie." Even car parking charges were included. All of this was paid for with Dorothea's money. Is there anything wrong with this picture?

Furthermore, in court, the family always claimed that Florida was a good place for Dorothea to be. They lived nearby and could keep in touch and visit her. But in the spring of 2021 Rosemary quit her teaching job in Florida and, I surmise, is now employed in Pennsylvania, where her daughter Megan now also resides and works. Dorothea's brother Ricky is a resident of Pennsylvania, while her nephew Michael lives in Texas. In 2021, there was no POA or Guardian or sibling in the vicinity of Dorothea's assisted living facility in Florida to keep an eye on her.

Early in March 2021, Rosemary purchased a house in Pennsylvania. But it wasn't until the beginning of August, a court order authorized her to move Dorothea from the Inspired Living Home in Florida to a facility in Pennsylvania. The Florida court approved her petition, and in September Dorothea was moved to Sunrise of North Wales in Pennsylvania.

Rosemary's petition included a request for $5,000 for the move; this was also approved. A request to transfer Rosemary's guardianship was provisionally accepted in January 2022; she would have to obtain an order from a Florida court to terminate her guardianship in that state.

I believe that Dorothea went to Inspired Living in Florida with just a week's worth of clothing, consistent with what she was wearing in photos posted online. Rosemary had sought reimbursement for a couple of hundred dollars for some items she bought for Dorothea's new "residence." What possible other possessions of Dorothea were moved to Pennsylvania that warranted such a high moving fee?

I can only speculate why Rosemary requested this move. Guardians usually reside in the state where their Wards are institutionalized. Once Rosemary worked and moved to Pennsylvania, would the state of Florida create trouble because no family members were left to monitor Dorothea? Did she move Dorothea to validate her guardianship in that new state?

I keep wondering what this move did to Dorothea. Old trees should not be transplanted. Being placed against her will in a facility must have been traumatic. Perhaps she adjusted and made new friends and acquaintances at Inspired Living before having to start all over in Pennsylvania. Did the move further make her feel that she had lost total control over her life?

In the meantime, there is still no way anyone can contact Dorothea. Since Rosemary had her declared incompetent, Dorothea has not even been allowed to speak over the phone with anyone who isn't pre-approved by Rosemary. Dorothea is completely isolated from former neighbors, friends, and former colleagues. Before June 2019 Dorothea was on the computer every day using her email. To date, no one has received any response from emails they sent her, and there have been no posts made on her Facebook page. Rosemary controls Dorothea's email account, and all regular mail to Dorothea is forwarded to Rosemary's address. I am surmising that Rosemary has done several "happy dances." In the meantime, she is being paid for being Dorothea's guardian. We don't know how much Rosemary is paid for her guardian services, but the average salary for a professional guardian in Florida is $40,000. I'm curious if she moved to Pennsylvania, if she continued to bill Dorothea for weekly or monthly visits. It would be something I would look into.

After I got hold of the bank's statements, I went over them with a fine-toothed comb. I sent a spread sheet of what I found to the agency overseeing financial fraud in guardianship cases in Florida. It doesn't appear it made its way into the court room. Of course, no one was contesting Dorothea's guardianship case, and I was still battling to have North Carolina drop the charges against me. It is something I want to pursue with the authorities.

My Court Case

Almost two years after my arrest, my court case has been caught in a web of postponements and continuances. I have not been able to face my accusers in a trial before a judge or a jury. The lackluster attitude of my defense lawyers and the failure of the police to request bank records or to interview new witnesses contributed to this. I felt the entire justice system had an ironclad grip on me and was just playing games with me in their continuances.

Flashback to May 2021 with my second lawyer, two years after my arrest. I finally believed we had made a step in the right direction. Sunset Beach Police subpoenaed the bank two times, eight months apart, for Dorothea's bank statements. They had previously failed to request ALL bank statements in the first subpoena. I was able to direct my lawyer to the specific amounts of money in the statements that Dorothea's family claimed they couldn't find; and therefore, they claimed I had stolen the money. It is important to note, in the North Carolina Department of Social Services report from June 2019, Rosemary told the social worker over the phone, that she had called the bank on June 17th and was informed that there was no missing money. All money remained in the bank, under Dorothea's name. Despite this knowledge, Rosemary filed the false police report against me for theft of $125K.

Following a meeting to review the bank statements with the ADA and their accountant, my lawyer called me announcing that he had some good news.

"Hello, Pam! I am ready to hand-deliver a letter to the Assistant District Attorney of North Carolina. I wanted to give you an overview of our position in your case before we give her the letter.

We are specifically addressing three allegations that are verifiably false."

"Are you sure she will listen to you? So far, she has ignored our attempts," I ventured.

"One way or another she will have to respond. It's an official document."

"Okay then, let's hear what you have to tell her."

"We will remind the Assistant District Attorney that you have consistently maintained your innocence, even to the point of declining a conditional discharge that would have resulted in the dismissal of your charges. You simply did not take any money from Dorothea or exploit her for any unlawful financial gain. Neither the state's indictment nor the Discovery specifically identified the funds that were supposedly diverted from Dorothea, so I will go through a list of issues that arose from Discovery and will therefore address them individually. I hope that this discussion will lead to the outright dismissal of all charges against you."

Breathing a sigh of relief, I said, "As Desmond Tutu said, 'Hope is being able to see that there is light despite all of the darkness.'"

My lawyer was silent. I had the feeling he had no idea who Tutu was. After a moment he responded, "First, there is a vague and unsupported allegation that you diverted funds from the Fidelity Investments account that contained well over 1 million dollars."

"But I never had any type of access to the Fidelity Investments account, nor did I ever attempt to gain access. The records of this account were never subpoenaed by Detective Cox during the investigation of this case. That means that there was no actual concern that funds were diverted from that account."

"As I said, Pam, it is a vague and unsupported allegation. Look, Pam, this entire case stems from Dorothea's family's desire to move Dorothea to a facility in Florida and take over her finances. They clearly viewed your close relationship to Dorothea as a threat to their plan. Their actions in this case showed that their strategy was to use false allegations against you to gain control. They have been successful in this effort: Rosemary was able to get her sister moved to Florida, place her in a facility that Rosemary began paying for with Dorothea's money (from an account that Dorothea had removed her sister from), and obtain guardianship over Dorothea through a court proceeding in Florida."

"I remember very clearly, that prior to my arrest Dorothea became very concerned about her sister's level of control over her finances and disagreed with her sister's plan to have her moved to a facility in Florida. She wrote a letter to that effect . . ."

My lawyer continued, "That letter is our Exhibit A and is included in our Discovery. It could be construed as evidence of Dorothea's intent to revoke her sister's state as POA. At the very least, the letter shows that Dorothea's primary concern was Rosemary's attempts to control her life and finances, and not any attempt on your part."

He delved deeper into the presentation further explaining, "After Dorothea was relocated to Florida, Rosemary moved forward with guardianship proceedings and gained control over Dorothea and her finances as guardian. All these records are publicly available. If there was any money diverted it would have surfaced in the guardianship proceedings. Additional court documents from the guardianship proceedings show that Rosemary sold Dorothea's house, valued at about $500,000."

After hearing him explain the case so succinctly, I needed to regain my composure.

"Are you still there, Pam?" he asked.

"Of course I am," I responded. "You exposed their devilish plan and how they succeeded so well with the help of the so-called protectors of the guardianship system. In the meantime, Dorothea is still languishing in a care facility, and I was jailed under their false accusations."

"Well, brace yourself, Pam. Rosemary's second allegation is that approximately $125,000 'disappeared' when two of Dorothea's bank accounts were "closed" in June, 2019. This is also a verifiably false allegation based on the information provided in Discovery. We will be able to show that none of Dorothea's money ever 'disappeared'; it was simply moved from accounts that Dorothea closed into new accounts with new account numbers."

"Dorothea took this step out of her own concern that her family members were about to try to move her to a home in Florida and take over her finances," I interjected.

My lawyer added, "On the afternoon of June 13, 2019, Rosemary had convinced Dorothea to add her to each of Dorothea's accounts as a joint account holder with right of survivorship. Exhibit C contains the signature cards showing Dorothea adding Rosemary as joint account holder on all three accounts on June 13, 2019. This was a very odd request from Rosemary, given that she already had a Durable Power of Attorney that would allow her access to such accounts in case Dorothea was declared incapacitated. But four days later, on June 17, 2019, Dorothea returned to the bank and opened three new accounts with sizeable balances."

"I am pretty sure that the total of those balances almost exactly match the amount that Rosemary falsely alleges was stolen," I interjected.

"Correct. The bank statements verify that the exact amount that was transferred out of the old accounts was deposited into the new accounts that were exclusively controlled by Dorothea; meaning absolutely no money was diverted or 'disappeared' as Rosemary alleged. Furthermore, you were never added to any of these accounts as a joint account holder or POA. Our Exhibit D contains the new signature cards showing only Dorothea as an authorized party for the new accounts. Exhibit E definitively establishes that the money was moved by Dorothea; it was not stolen."

"From what I have seen coming from this ADA, she will find something to circumvent all this evidence." I said.

"Possibly," he retorted, "but it's still bank records' evidence. There is a third allegation about the car Dorothea sold. Rosemary alleges that Dorothea was somehow deprived of the money from the car sale. We have an image of the check issued by CarMax that was deposited in Dorothea's savings account the day after the sale. The bank statements for that account also reflect that this money was deposited and remained there. This, again, is a verifiably false allegation based on the information available in Discovery."

"There are a couple more things I have to mention, Pam. First the family questioned the Christmas check Dorothea gave you for $5,000. Dorothea considered it a valid gift to you by noting 'Happy Holidays' in the memo line. I will tell the ADA that Dorothea has the right to spend her money as she wishes. If the family wants to assert that Dorothea was incompetent to give a gift of her own money they will also have to explain how Dorothea repeatedly wrote checks for holiday gifts to her family members, often bearing the same note in the memo line. None of these checks were forged ones, including your Christmas gift. The only forged checks in this entire case were forged by Rosemary or another family member who had gained access to Dorothea's finances after your arrest. Exhibit G shows genuine checks bearing Dorothea's signature as well as forged checks that began to be used in July 2019. Each of these forged

134

checks was written on Dorothea's new account, which was one of the accounts that Dorothea had created to remove Rosemary as joint account holder the month prior."

I added, "This last information is new to me. But it does not surprise me. I keep wondering what else we will find out once the books will be opened about Rosemary's management of Dorothea's guardianship."

At least, my lawyer had made an honest attempt to present my case and had the Discoveries to support his arguments. Deep down, however, I was still doubtful. I had been let down too many times in the last two years and wanted to protect myself against another disappointment.

Unfortunately, I had been right feeling that way. In July 2021, about two months after my lawyer delivered the letter, the ADA responded. They acknowledged that I didn't actually take any money. They, however, issued a new indictment based on the statute that states that it is illegal to "endeavor to obtain."

This statute, covering the exploitation of an elder adult or disabled adult, states: "It is unlawful for a person: (i) who stands in a position of trust and confidence with an elder adult or disabled adult, or (ii) who has a business relationship with an elder adult or disabled adult to knowingly, by deception or intimidation, obtain or use, or endeavor to obtain or use, an elder adult's or disabled adult's funds, assets, or property with the intent to temporarily or permanently deprive the elder adult or disabled adult of the use, benefit, or possession of the funds, assets, or property, or to benefit someone other than the elder adult or disabled adult."

So, ADA Shirley Smircic, agreed that I did not steal any money but now claimed that I "intended" to steal the money. They would have to prove that everything I did for Dorothea was geared towards obtaining access to her assets.

Worth mentioning here is that it was a Grand Jury that had to approve this new indictment. Grand juries review the evidence of criminal wrongdoing and issue an indictment, or a True Bill, if they conclude that the evidence was sufficient. Based on the statements made by Sunset Beach Police, the Grand Jury decided that the evidence presented, established probable cause and issued an indictment against me.

One of the most common criticisms of grand juries is that they have become too dependent on prosecutors. Instead of looking at the evidence presented to them, grand juries are simply issuing the indictment that the prosecutors ask them to issue. Critics charge that a grand jury typically rubber-stamps the prosecution's moves, indicting anyone the prosecutor cares to bring before it. Unlike a preliminary hearing, held in court with the defense side present, a grand jury is prosecutor friendly. It should also be mentioned that grand jury proceedings are secret. I will never know what "evidence" was presented to the grand jury that resulted in an indictment.

In early August 2021, I sent my lawyer a series of questions. He had advised me earlier to plea bargain, but I was determined that under no circumstances would I do this as I am completely innocent. My future, my reputation, my job, all relied on the proof of my innocence. When he answered my questions, he again strongly suggested that I consider a plea bargain, as he said it was the only way to guarantee a dismissal of my charges. He was shocked at my refusal of the deal and said that in his entire career, he had never had a client turn down such a favorable plea offer.

I always thought that a plea bargain could hamper my ability to maintain a civil case against a defendant at the end of this process. Although he acknowledged that this might be true, he opined that my chances of success in any civil action for malicious prosecution were quite low. He warned me that it might be challenging to find a capable civil attorney willing to take on my case because of a low likelihood of financial recovery. And at no time did he ever advise me of any kind of statute of limitations regarding a counter lawsuit, when I repeatedly told him I wanted to file a defamation lawsuit against Rosemary and the other family members involved.

My lawyer finally promised to make all possible effort on my behalf if I insisted on proceeding to trial against his advice. He did, however, not believe going to trial was worth the risk given the favorable deal I had been offered. But the decision was mine to make.

Accepting a plea bargain would have gone against everything in my soul. It would say that I was in some way guilty of endeavoring to harm Dorothea. It might also discourage people to help another person, fearful of becoming an object of suspicion.

Later in August 2021, ADA Shirley Smircic produced a "superseding indictment," charging that I "knowingly, by deception endeavored to obtain or use the funds, assets, and property of Dorothea." They added that the value of the funds, assets, and property was about $124,000. So, they would try to prove that I intended to obtain that money, even if it had never been missing. A trial date was set for January 28, and less than 7 days later, another prosecutor's continuance was granted with February 28 re-scheduled as the new trial date.

If found guilty of a Class G felony, I could end up in state prison for 10 years and pay up to $25,000. Furthermore, a felony charge or felony conviction would never be expunged from a criminal record. There would be no chance to be hired again in the sectors I had worked in because they would not hire anyone with a felony record. Finally, I would be prevented from owning a gun, traveling outside the country, or voting.

Was it not enough that I had spent time in jail on trumped- up charges? Now the superseding indictment could screw up the remainder of my life and that made me mad as hell. More than ever, I was determined to fight them and regain my reputation. Or better, I was going to fight them to regain my life!

With the superseding indictment, my lawyer sent a new contract with an additional fee of $10,000 to move forward with the trial. I decided not to renew his contract because I felt he believed more in my settling with a plea bargain than proving my innocence. Now I had to find a new lawyer who believed in me and would lead me on a journey towards vindication.

The Views of Dorothea's Family

To this point I have described what happened to Dorothea and to me in this memoir. You have become familiar with some of Dorothea's family members because of their involvement with Dorothea and their success in placing her in an assisted living facility. It was also her family who caused my arrest, which led to my battle to prove my innocence.

To understand what Dorothea's family said and did we had to rely on court cases and the records of their petitions for guardianship. All this information is in the public domain and has been duly reported and examined in the foregoing pages.

In a story like this it is always important to consider the two sides of the problem. A critic of my story could argue that Dorothea's family did not have the chance to show how they felt about her situation and about the reasons why they did what they did. Although throughout the story there are some glimpses describing how they felt, one could argue that the family did not have the chance to tell their side of the story. Due to the verifiably false allegations, I seriously doubt that the family would be willing to be interviewed about their actions, without further defamation to my character. Any such attempt would have to wait until all legal issues are resolved.

The only direct information is three letters written by Dorothea's younger brother Ricky and her nephew Michael. These letters were written in July 2019 after Dorothea had been confined in the care facility in Florida. The letters became part of the public record and Discovery.

The letters offer a detailed timeline of their activities and events, as they perceived them. They depict in great detail what the family did during the days just before my arrest and after they brought

Dorothea back to North Carolina and ultimately to the assisted living facility in Florida. They describe the feelings the family had about me as Dorothea's caregiver for two years after Mary Anne died.

Their mention of "emotional stress" and "financial distress" in these letters, certainly expresses some of their feelings. Both Michael and Ricky repeatedly try to show how close the family was to Dorothea as their sister and aunt: the visits to Maryland, and North Carolina, the presence of Dorothea at main events in their youth, and the closeness to both Dorothea and Rosemary's family Their expressions of concern for their "dear Auntie" are ubiquitous. Why then did they not visit her when she spent a year in an apartment?

I also found it odd that Ricky and Michael were the most important actors in those days of June. Rosemary is barely mentioned although she seemed to be the mastermind behind the entire saga. It should also be noted that there is no mention of Rosemary and Megan's visit to North Carolina in June 2019.

The timeline of the months of June and July, was developed in a previous chapter mirroring closely the timeline in their letters. Yet, the many fallacies, misrepresentations and plain lies that appear in the letters, repeating the charges against me used in Rosemary's petitions for guardianship earlier, made me decide not to include their letters verbatim. I just want to summarize some of the things they state about me as the "great conniver."

They said that I lied about being Dorothea's student; that I lied when promising to live with Dorothea; that I lied to the police and to the family about her deteriorating condition. They said that I made sure to get control of Dorothea's finances by, among other things, learning her computer passwords, setting up her bill paying, and attempting to become her POA. They stated that I tried to alienate the family from Dorothea by: setting up security cameras that I completely controlled, by warning Dorothea about her family in emails, and by preventing the family from contacting Dorothea.

140

I hope that foregoing chapters have shown that all these allegations were pure fantasy. But these allegations became charges of wrongdoing and "exploitation" and were used by Rosemary to have me arrested. If they really believed in these allegations, it is no wonder that they considered me a threat and Enemy Number One.

In the end, we don't have to imagine what the motivations of the family were in this entire process. In other words, we don't have to imagine what "the other side" was thinking.

From the early days after Mary Anne's death, it became obvious that Rosemary and her family wanted Dorothea in a care facility so that they had control over her and her finances. In order to do this, they had to make everyone believe that she had dementia and could not take care of herself. They also had to make everyone believe that I was a threat who could prevent them from accomplishing their plans; so, they had to eliminate me. They succeeded in this by placing Dorothea in a care facility and by charging me with the crime of exploitation.

It is also obvious that, from the very beginning, Dorothea was afraid that her sister was up to no good. She repeatedly let the family know that her only goal was to retire in her house in North Carolina and expressed that she had no interest in going to Florida or anywhere else for that matter. At the same time, she attempted to keep a civil relationship with her family by visits and sending regular checks for special occasions. But when a friend of mine, who was at Mary Anne's funeral, asked Dorothea how her family was doing, Dorothea curtly answered, "They don't care!"

Dorothea's family has abundantly shown that they did not have the best interest in mind for their sister and aunt. If they had, they would now be able to visit Dorothea in her dream house in North Carolina.

In the Afterword of his book, *The Wolf is at the Door,* Michael Hackard astutely describes how we can decide to be treated if we find ourselves in a position of vulnerability.

"We do not need to have incapacity to be vulnerable. Our particular vulnerability might be caused through illness, disability, injury, age, education, emotional distress, isolation, or dependency. Whatever vulnerability, we will ultimately rely on those who apply the Golden Rule (Do unto others as you would have them do unto you) to protect us when we cannot protect ourselves. We will be thankful for those souls who risk scorn and controversy to oppose wrongdoing."[16]

---

[16] Michael Hackard, Esq. *The Wolf is at the Door,* p.133

Vindication!

While Dorothea is still silently suffering in her separation from neighbors and friends in an assisted living facility in Pennsylvania, my story took an unexpected, yet long anticipated turn in January 2022.

It had gotten so bad that at every turn in the case, and after every communication with the ADA, I would anxiously wait for yet another shoe to drop, another accusation to be piled on their wildly long list. In ADA Shirley Smircic's last ditch efforts to pad her stats and wiggle out of an unwarranted prosecution, the Assistant District Attorney's office had sent a duplicate of the plea bargain, that she had shopped in front of my previous attorney, hoping I would accept it from the new attorneys. Knowing that the thought of stealing funds from Dorothea had never crossed my mind, I remained steadfast and refused.

To my new team of lawyers in North Carolina I presented the facts, the paperwork, the videos, the recordings, and all the court filings. They spent two months interviewing teachers, students, neighbors, and others, to prepare the facts, interviews, depositions, and affidavits. These were presented to the ADA prior to the scheduled hearing date in late February.

Hours after the presentation, my new lawyer called and told me that the presentation had been well received by the ADA, but that he could not promise anything. After years of continuances and lack of action from my previous lawyers who failed to investigate the mounds of supporting evidence, against any of the accusations, I was not expecting that I would be vindicated.

The following day, I was preparing breakfast in the kitchen when my lawyer phoned me again.

"Pam, an hour ago, I received an email from the ADA telling me that she was filing for dismissal of your case."

I had to gasp for air and almost dropped the phone. It had been such a rollercoaster for almost three years that, although I wanted to jump up and down, I was in shock. My legs were weak as I walked down the few steps to my basement and sat down on the 1956 green speckled, asbestos tiled floor and started to cry.

"Thank you so much for all the work you and your team did," I managed to say. "I want you to know, that I recognize just how much time, effort and mental capability it took to go through so much documentation and grasp all nuances within the mounds of evidence that proved the accusations false. I recognize you and your team accomplished that in a very short time frame. I am beyond appreciative of your belief in me and my innocence. I am forever indebted to you for believing in me."

Still shaking, I went back upstairs to the kitchen, where my mom was waiting for breakfast.

"Mom, I just got a call from my lawyer. The ADA is filing for dismissal of my charges."

She looked as stunned as I had been when I heard the news. "Thank God, our prayers were heard!" she whispered while we were embracing, tears of joy welling in our eyes.

My lawyer told me later that all charges would be dismissed "with prejudice." This meant that nobody could charge me again at a later date. With a recently passed law, the process was accompanied by an automatic expungement, so there should be no record of my case within the state of North Carolina court system.

Unfortunately, a couple of dark clouds remain in the sky. As yet there is no hardcopy document stating that, in fact, the charges are dismissed. When anyone asks me for documentation, the only thing I can present is the email from my lawyer where the ADA said that she "was filing for dismissal." As for follow-up, several weeks later, my lawyer researched my case, and couldn't find anything within the North Carolina court system. I still feel a gnawing hesitancy to actually believe that it happened.

In addition, the article in the North Carolina newspaper about my arrest that I mentioned above, remains accessible on the Internet, and my case remains logged in the National Crime Information Center, and a local case search in the Maryland courts, still shows a warrant for my arrest and will never be removed, unless I pay for the removal of the action from public view.

For nearly three years, I had been fighting to prove my innocence. From the beginning I knew that the family and their lawyers, the courts, and the police had created false allegations against me. After nearly three years of lawyers' fees, over a week spent incarcerated in a jail, and the continuous accusations of theft, elder abuse and exploitation, the truth has finally set me free.

We don't know yet what this development will mean for the guardianship Rosemary and her family have over Dorothea. They did use false charges against me in order to obtain that guardianship to "protect Dorothea." Now that these charges have been proven to be groundless, should the family continue to have power over Dorothea?

With the dismissal of the charges against me, I can end this saga. I won. But did Dorothea? Other chapters might have to be written: Will Dorothea's family be able to keep their guardianship? Will Dorothea be able to retire in a place of her own choosing? Will Dorothea ever regain her constitutional rights? Can the police and the ADA be charged with malicious prosecution, or mishandling of a vulnerable adult whose welfare they were ultimately responsible?

Recent court documents about Rosemary's management of the guardianship show that she was getting approved for charges on

Dorothea's credit card which did not benefit Dorothea: a subscription to the *New York Times,* a newspaper never favored by Dorothea; a satellite radio for a car: but, Dorothea no longer has a car; and more than a year's worth of payments for Wi-Fi, cable TV, and a landline in the North Carolina house after Dorothea moved to the assisted living facility.

The court in Florida, however, even after an audit, failed to deem these charges suspicious, and approved the reporting of Rosemary's charges. Without an investigation, and relying merely on the word of the guardian they appointed, they consented to her request to move Dorothea to Pennsylvania and establish a guardianship in that state.

In the end, I have prevailed, to some extent. But has total justice been done? For nearly three years I have grown increasingly doubtful about the justice practiced in the courts and in law enforcement. I will do everything in my power to make sure that what happened to me does not happen to anyone else.

The first step I have taken is to have this distributed to the authorities that can investigate such egregious, malicious premeditated actions against an innocent person, and an elderly person. May it make people aware that the story of Dorothea and me is repeated every day in all corners of the United States. And if it happened to me, a volunteer firefighter, and auxiliary police officer, a full-time state fire safety inspector, with a long history of selfless giving within her community of friends, neighbors and co-workers, it can happen to anyone. Don't think it can't. The FBI reports that in 2021 alone there were 24,000 victims of elder abuse scams totaling a loss of $1 billion. For every law that has good intentions, there are people out there who will find a way to use, abuse and twist it in a manner that was never intended.

I do not know what will come next, but I do know that the people who harmed Dorothea, and the people who jumped on board

146

without any evidence of wrong doing, to help those harming Dorothea, and who unjustly prosecuted me, must be held accountable, and must pay restitution to all who were harmed. If this happens, the guardianship system will have taken a positive step forward.

Total justice will not have been done until Dorothea is living in a place she chooses herself, has been reimbursed for the money wrongfully taken from her, has regained her civil rights, and has reclaimed her shattered retirement dreams.

As a parting gift, I want to share with you some of the hard lessons I learned in this entire process.

I don't ever regret having assisted Dorothea, and I will continue to help people in need whenever I meet them. But perhaps this is the right moment to share the lessons I learned about helping a person in need. My simple advice is, be true to yourself, always tell the truth. Truth is easy to remember and doesn't change. Do not give up on humanity, but (CYA) cover your ass. Thank goodness, I didn't delete emails, or phone records, or texts. I used credit cards and debit cards to purchase gas, and merchandise which proved my travel and travel dates. I used Amazon for purchases; it recorded the dates and kept a history of items I bought. You now know the dangers of those who may accuse you of wrongdoing. You now know how authority in the wrong hands can and will work against you, no matter how nice a person you are, how much volunteer work you have done over your lifetime, or how selfless you are in any given situation. People can and may take advantage of you. People who do not know you will believe horrible gossip and may take action against you, on an emotional level, based on the gossip they hear, without demanding any proof to back up the horrible story as true, they may throw you under the bus. Horrible people will ruin your life. It is imperative that you associate with good-hearted, well-intentioned, emotionally and mentally mature friends and acquaintances. Always take the high road. Listen to those good little guardian angels sitting on your shoulders guiding you along the better path of humanity. Ignore the temptations to off-road morally, causing harm to yourself and/or to others around you, even if it sounds like fun, or that you could benefit, (at the detriment of another). Know that it could be used against you, further down that same road. I have my parents and teachers to thank for instilling these ideals in me, along my life journey. I have lived my life in the best manner I could, helping friends, and even strangers along the way, because that is who I am.

This was the most difficult four years of my life. I look back, and I don't know how I survived; there were many very dark days. I am so very grateful to my friends, family, former teachers, and classmates who believed in me, who listened ... over and over, and over again, and over and over and over. I am forever in your debt. In the past, after hearing a news report of someone's pending legal issues, I easily brushed it off saying, "Eh, they will work it all out in the courts." After my experience, I will never say that again. I have a deep empathy for anyone stuck in the court system. It is broken beyond repair, in my opinion. Cronyism between law enforcement, lawyers and judges runs rampant. Many states do not even have "speedy trial" laws, and when they are challenged, the person is let go after months or years of incarceration, only to be re-charged and re- incarcerated, so that the broken process begins all over from square one. Innocent people are losing everything they own, including all their savings trying to defend themselves. Those ads you see, "You don't pay if we don't win..." Defending yourself isn't a for profit court case. Those lawyers won't take your case, unless you pay them up front. It's a hefty price. Don't expect a public defender to do any investigations on your behalf either. They have 800 other poor people to defend, so, take a number.

If it wasn't for my family's support, I would be wrongfully convicted, due to horrible legal representation, zero police investigation, misleading and malicious prosecution. Or I'd be homeless living under a bridge, because the charges got me terminated from my job, and everything I owned was repossessed because of the ADA's intentional continuances were granted without being contested, needlessly extending my period of unemployment due to baseless felony charges. Or sadly, I'd be dead because the deep depression of hopelessness, brought on by the broken court system, failed to protect me, ruined my life, my reputation, and foreseeable future, and instead claimed my life. They aren't seeking the truth; they are seeking a conviction. My prolonged case proves it.

I can't claim racial injustice. Our failed legal justice system has gone beyond that. We have to recognize that policy and procedure with regard to law enforcement and the courts are being tossed aside regarding everyone's rights. Authority is in the wrong hands, and these individuals are not being held accountable. Prosecutorial, Qualified and Absolute immunity for anyone and everyone needs to be changed, or outright removed from the books immediately. All people, without regard to their job or position in society, must be held liable for their actions.

I was very naive, finding myself in the broken court system. How could the police lie? How could you get indicted without actual evidence? How does an Evidentiary Hearing have no evidence? How does evidence disappear? How do police ignore investigating evidence that is brought to their attention? Why would police mislead the court, or falsify a reason for an arrest? What do they gain by not seeking the truth? I expected the glossy textbook constitutional court room we all learned about. "Tell the truth, the whole truth, and nothing but the truth." It was a very rude awakening. Sadly, it is routinely accepted by law enforcement, lawyers and judges and not to be challenged by all who enter, at the expense of the innocent.

Many people now just cannot accept that there are people who are willing to help others without any expectation of reward. All the silent good Samaritans who came to the rescue on 9/11 and after school shootings, hurricanes, and national disasters prove otherwise. I wish I could say with complete confidence, if you do this, you will be

149

able to identify "the wolf at the door", but there are no guarantees. Prepare for the worst, hope for the best, and take some law courses before you need them.

In March 2022, shortly after charges were dropped against me, I presented a lengthy letter with documented evidence to the Sunset Beach N.C. police chief Ken Klamar proving that Rosemary and Michael had filed a false police report. I requested charges be brought against them.

In May of 2022, Chief Klamar's response to me was that he consulted ADA Shirley Smircic (the same ADA who indicted me twice without any evidence of wrong doing) and she determined there wasn't enough probable cause to move forward to charge Rosemary and Michael. His response added insult to injury. Solid documented evidence of lying to the police, and filing a false police report was placed right in his hands and he failed to act to protect me, again. There are multiple times where the civil liberties of Dorothea and me have been, not only ignored but stomped on and drug though the mud. This true story needs to be fully investigated by the Department of Justice. The abuse and miscarriage of justice initiated by the Sunset Beach Police Detective Jarod Cox, Detective Stan Gurgunus, and advanced by Assistant Chief Joe Smith and then acted on by ADA Shirley Smircic, needs to be stopped so more innocent people do not have their lives destroyed and life savings eliminated defending themselves against corrupt cops and inexperienced ADAs furthering their careers. This results in both incompetent ADAs and police hiding behind, and using the statutes of limitations, and immunity as their defense. This abuse of authority has to stop. They need to be held accountable, something needs to be in place to make them behave honestly, investigate fully, and seek the truth in these cases. They did none of this for me or Dorothea. The truth was not hiding, it was not difficult to find. They simply ignored it, and then intentionally mislead others, in the hopes they'd get away with it. They did not care whose life they destroyed. Finding the truth did not matter to them.

This experience made me aware of the inequities in the justice system. Someone without my education, and without financial and emotional support from family and friends has an almost impossible chance at navigating the court system successfully on their own. It is heavily stacked against them. This has got to change.

An Epilogue

I have asked my mentor and friend to share with me some of the personal thoughts that emerged from the review of this remarkable and convoluted story. I believe the following monologue is an appropriate epilogue to this story. This is what was said to me:

"I knew Dorothea and Mary Anne for more than two decades as friends and colleagues at Notre Dame Prep. I remember Mary Anne as a gentle soul with a constant smile, as a teacher, as one who made it to the highest echelons in the health care industry, and as a faithful friend of Dorothea.

Among her colleagues at school, Dorothea was respected as an excellent teacher. Everybody knew she was demanding but fair; an educator who continuously challenged her students.

Over the years, I learned that Dorothea was a giving person. During the yearly pasta fundraiser for Filipino schoolchildren at Notre Dame Prep, she always helped in the kitchen, and then she'd make a donation for the cause. I was not surprised to learn that she and Mary Anne supported a long list of charities.

After my retirement from Notre Dame Prep, we kept in touch, but met only occasionally. When Mary Anne passed away in 2017, I could not attend her funeral, but my spouse represented me at the funeral Mass.

In January 2018, Dorothea appeared again at the pasta fundraiser. As she had done in the past, she helped in the kitchen and left a hefty donation for the charity drive. That was the last time I saw Dorothea.

While expressing my concern for Dorothea after several unsuccessful attempts to get in touch with her, a former colleague asked me if I could help you organize and tell your story. I did not know you as a student, but had met you a few times while you were teaching in the Middle School.

In the midst of the Covid pandemic, we arranged to meet at my house. We sat in the enclosed back porch, both properly masked. I listened to you for close to four hours, telling me what you and Dorothea had endured since Mary Anne's death. It was the first time that I learned that Dorothea's family had managed to place her in an assisted living facility after she moved to her house in North Carolina to enjoy her retirement.

Your story touched me deeply. When you asked me if I would be willing to guide you in retelling your experiences, I agreed without hesitation. Dorothea and Mary Anne had been good friends and colleagues for years. I empathized with Dorothea who was now in an assisted living facility. From the beginning, I also felt that an incredible injustice had been done to you and that your story had to be told.

I knew my previous publishing experiences would be helpful to you in accomplishing your goals. But I was in unfamiliar territory regarding guardianships, and we were about to tackle a real challenge that would involve a lot of research.

My spouse, who had worked for more than three decades with senior citizens as a social worker, became a rich source of information.

You provided thousands of pages of documentation about your relationship with Dorothea, your communications, the things you did for her, the traveling, the meetings that took place. Your extensive documentation grew with each avenue pursued in your quest to prove your innocence against the convoluted charges of elder abuse.

In the above chapters, a timeline of the events to better organize this complex story. In doing so, an attempt was made to expose the perils of the broken guardian system in this country.

Dorothea's life and yours were existentially affected by the events described. Not only did you spend over a week in jail, but your unpleasant dilemma of legal troubles also continued, something that you did not deserve. Now, for almost three years, Dorothea has potentially been languishing in institutions of which she had intended to avoid at all costs.

There are more than the two storylines outlined in this saga. The material presented here is only a small portion of the complexities, lawlessness and the failure to follow policy and procedure, that took place in the courts, by the family, and by law enforcement. You chose to tackle just two, the first of which is how Dorothea's family managed to place her in an assisted living facility. I have never met Rosemary and her family, however by mentoring you, and reviewing the series of events that took place, it has given me a clear picture of their personalities.

Very soon after Mary Anne's passing, Rosemary decided that Dorothea could become a great source of income and set in motion a plan to achieve this by any means possible. The above chapters describe how she succeeded in her endeavors.

The second storyline involves you assisting Dorothea and ending up being charged with elder abuse. It is obvious that Rosemary did not want you to get in the way of her plans. Notwithstanding your good intentions and your life-long habit of helping people in need, the family was suspicious of your relationship with her in general, and assumed you controlled Dorothea's bank accounts. Your ongoing monthly trips to Sunset Beach seemed unreasonable to them, and they suspected that you were trying to replace Mary Anne in Dorothea's life and, by doing so, would deepen the tumultuous wedge already established between the family and

Dorothea. That is why they repeatedly portrayed you as a liar and as someone who intended to financially profit from your relationship with Dorothea by gradually immersing yourself into Dorothea's life.

Some people might question the objectivity of this story. I would have loved to hear Dorothea's side of the story, but this was not possible. All Dorothea's contacts with the outside world, email, phone, and online access, are controlled by Rosemary. We don't know what Dorothea's present physical health or state of mind is; all of this might only be revealed if, and when Dorothea is released from the assisted living facility.

We are still mostly in the dark about the way Rosemary is managing the guardianship. Although public court records describe certain events, the details of the guardianship management are almost impossible to come by and may be sequestered by the courts.

Up until this point, interviewing family members or Dorothea herself has been impossible, and I don't foresee any opportunity to do this.

You have not had an easy time writing this story. Throughout the process, the aim was for accuracy in presenting the facts as they occurred. Dorothea's story revealed some of the complexities of the human soul and its dark corners: the power of money and greed, the ease with which the truth is sometimes bent, the existence of lawyers without a conscience, and the fragility of family relationships and of human institutions such as the guardianship courts.

This story has also revealed some of the bright corners of the human soul: the quest for justice and truth, selfless compassion and charity towards others, and the uniqueness of every human being.

The heavily documented story of Dorothea and you, Pam, is a warning to all elderly people who are not legally prepared for the possibility that they may become incapacitated in the waning years of their life. They will have to deal with a guardianship system that does not have a stellar reputation for protecting the rights of seniors in our society.

It is also a story about how careful one must be when volunteering to help someone in need. Compassion can not only be misinterpreted, but there are those who will quickly, intentionally and maliciously make false assumptions. Instead of being thanked for your kindness, you might be punished.

Your writing of this story has also made my spouse and me more aware of our own situation as seniors. Because of our age and medical problems, we sometimes must rely on the kindness of friends and strangers. We might enjoy living in a retirement facility, but doing so would mean leaving the comfort of a home we have occupied for more than fifty years. We are faced with difficult decisions about how we will spend our remaining years. More than ever, I have become aware of how, as a senior, I am an easy target for scammers and people who are trying to steal my identity.

Your story made me reflect on everyone's lot in life: the fact of aging. If we are fortunate enough to live for many decades, we all face getting old. Although there are challenges to being a senior, there are benefits too. It is satisfying to be liberated from the daily rat race, to enjoy our children and grandchildren, to relish the companionship of old friends, to take up hobbies we never had the time to pursue before, and to feel secure with our Social Security and pension checks.

Taking it a step further, as senior citizens, we become increasingly aware that life is transitory, and we develop a tendency to look back. We know we no longer have the time to fashion a new future, and so we tend to hold on to our memories. People who were once vital to our world have disappeared, our contemporaries are passing away, and we become slowly, but surely alone in the world.

We sometimes get the feeling that getting old means that we are losing something on a daily basis. We are conscious that at the end of this fleeting life stands death. If we believe in an afterlife, eternity is at the door. If we are not believers, death leads to either nothingness, or the opportunity to do it all over again.

At this ripe old age, we have seen ideas and trends being born and then disappear. Moral dictates that seemed unshakable have lost their power. Standards about right and wrong have given up their robust command and have been replaced by new standards. Gradually, our old views have widened out. We let go of convictions that we have promoted and defended for ages, and we open up to new views.

Is this the "wisdom of the ages" consistently ascribed to old people? Is it insight into "things as they are," an insight that is gained only when one nears the end?

At the time of this writing, the world is still in shock from the Coronavirus pandemic. More than ever, in the last two years we have become aware of how fragile human life is and how much we take things for granted: the wonderful feeling of a hug, the dedication of a nurse, the joy of a day at the beach, the thrill of Major League Baseball, or the ease of international travel. We should remind ourselves how lucky we are to have food, running water, and electricity while millions in the world live on a dollar a day and are deprived of life's basic necessities.

The world is reeling from the Russian invasion of the Ukraine. Never did I think that, after growing up as a child in World War II, I would be faced with the possibility of a third world war in my old age.

Old age is also a time of deterioration for our mind and body. It is a time when our circle of friends and coworkers gradually becomes smaller, when the pharmacy becomes our most visited establishment, when we are grateful to have traveled abroad when younger, when we are hoping to share our acquired wisdom with younger generations, or when, God forbid, we become victims of scams or the greed of family members.

I can only imagine what Dorothea thinks of getting older. The few joys of aging have probably been denied her. She is separated from her friends and acquaintances, has been removed from her intended retirement home, and is trapped in an assisted living facility she did not want, surrounded by people she does not know. Is she holding on to her memories, knowing that her future looks bleak? Does she have any remaining hope that one day her nightmare will end?

Until the day Dorothea can move to a place of her choosing, she remains a victim of her family's greed and the broken guardianship system.

Collaborating on this story has been a revelation for both of us. I have become more aware of the problems of aging and the way other people are trying to take advantage of it. Your story has guarded me against people who might use U.S. institutions and laws to control how I live my life. I thank you for this increased awareness.

I can only hope that the publication of your story protects at least one more person against the claws of greedy relatives. Hopefully, it will prevent at least one more person from being falsely accused.

I would like to end my thoughts to you with a quote from one of my favorite Roman orators, Marcus Tullius Cicero's essay "On Old Age" ("De Senectute"): "We who have aged have been tested and endured, failed and persevered, were rejected and survived. We learn to live with gratitude. The good we did will endure forever."

Acknowledgments

My mentor and friend has succeeded in helping me to reveal the truth in presenting the facts in a captivating and succinct way. It was the oversight I needed to harness the raw, hopeless emotions, that I carried with me, and turn them into a head-strong passion to fight an injustice, not only for myself but for others. I was able to express my innermost feelings, frustrations, hopes and sorrows; expressions that have never come easy for me to share.

I do hope that this book becomes a warning to all elderly people that "the wolf is at the door" and assists their relatives in protecting them from predatory guardians.

An unexpected friendship developed with my mentor during the research for this manuscript. I never told him, but I avoided his classes in high school, because I thought he had the reputation of being tough and demanding. What I learned was that his ability to comprehend complex dynamics and provide insightful feedback had not faded over time. I'm not sure he's as tough as I imagined, but he is demanding of himself.

I am grateful to the many people over the years, who agreed to read the manuscript while in development, and gave their constructive comments. I decided to shield their identities until I deem it is safe and have their approval to acknowledge their participation. The last thing I want to have happen is have my friends experience the financial ruin I experienced, due to frivolous retaliatory acts by others.

As this manuscript heads to print, my defamation case against the family was struck down in District Court of Maryland, the ruling being that each time I learned of additional lies being told by the family, in August of 2017, June 2019, March 2020, and February 2022 each date had exceeded the statute of limitations when I filed the case in 2022. Ten months, and nearly 70 exhibits of documented statements of defamation submitted into the case, I waited for the judge to rule on the Statute of Limitations and on the motion by the defense that the false statements to police are privileged testimony. My requests for subpoenas proving premeditation against me, were denied, because as a pro se plaintiff, you must wait for a Scheduling Hearing to be set by the judge. Over the past four years, even with all the undeniable evidence in my and Dorothea's defense, this has languished in multiple courts, and no one has been held accountable for their actions, and defamatory statements. Shattered Dreams focuses on the broken and easily manipulated Guardianship system in the United States, as it offers only a glimpse, just one fourth of what transpired on one level of this human tragedy. This story has not ended, not by a long shot; there has to be accountability by those who violated our civil liberties.

To recapitulate, the three prongs of injustice related in this memoir are the following:

1. The injustice of being a victim of a false police report and the consequences that ensued.

2. The injustice of law enforcement failing to follow policy and procedure, failing to fully investigate allegations made, failing to secure evidence in an effort to cover up their wrong doing, and their support of the false police report.

3. The injustice of the courts to provide compensation for deliberate and outright defamation and malicious prosecution of innocent persons that lead to the false imprisonment, and for Dorothea, the loss of property and loss of all rights, including voting rights through forced guardianship.

Much more needs to be brought out into the light, disclosed and exposed, to prevent the courts and accusers from continuing to harm other innocent people who are just like me and Dorothea.

I am forever indebted to the many friends and family members who have patiently listened to me throughout this ordeal and who have stood by my side. You have been a tremendous support; I never would have made it alone.

Finally, my heartfelt appreciation goes to my editors who are accomplished writers and English connoisseurs, for working wonders with the manuscript. The attention to detail and the constructive comments made the text more focused and engaging.

eee

.

Made in the USA
Middletown, DE
20 September 2023

38685431R00089